Lost Voices

Gilda O'Neill was born and brought up in the East End. She left school at fifteen but returned to education as a mature student. She is the author of fourteen novels and has also had six non-fiction books published including the highly-acclaimed *Sunday Times* bestsellers, *My East End* and *Our Street*. She is a full-time writer and lives in East London with her husband and family.

Praise for Gilda O'Neill

'A treasure . . . Every page is a delight. Every chapter made vivid by a writer who has poured heart and soul into her book'
Daily Mail

'A cracking read'
Martina Cole

'A rich tapestry . . . a finely detailed examination of our not so distant past. Her book is as much a piece of history as the accounts it contains'
Time Out

'A compelling and menacing page-turner'
Daily Express

'A sharp eye, a warm heart and a gift for storytelling'
Elizabeth Buchan

'Her vivid, flint-edged picture of London's East End in the sixties leaps off the page with its sardonic dialogue and sharply realised characters . . . you'll find it very difficult indeed to put this one down'
Crime Time

Also by Gilda O'Neill

FICTION
The Cockney Girl
Whitechapel Girl
The Bells of Bow
Just Around the Corner
Cissie Flowers
Dream On
The Lights of London
Playing Around
Getting There
The Sins of Their Fathers
Make Us Traitors
Of Woman Born
Rough Justice
Secrets of the Heart

NON-FICTION
A Night Out With The Girls: Women Having a Good Time
My East End: Memories of Life in Cockney London
Our Street: East End Life in the Second World War
The Good Old Days: Crime, Murder and Mayhem in Victorian London
East End Tales (Quick Reads)

Lost Voices

Memories of a Vanished
Way of Life

Gilda O'Neill

arrow books

Published by Arrow Books 2006

4 6 8 10 9 7 5

Gilda O'Neill has asserted her right under the Copyright, Designs and
Patents Act, 1988 to be identified as the author of this work

First published in Great Britain in 1990 by
The Women's Press Limited, as *Pull No More Bines*

Arrow Books
Random House, 20 Vauxhall Bridge Road,
London SW1V 2SA

www.rbooks.co.uk

Addresses for companies within The Random House Group Limited
can be found at: www.randomhouse.co.uk/offices.htm

The Random House Group Limited Reg. No. 954009

A CIP catalogue record for this book
is available from the British Library

ISBN 9780099498360

The Random House Group Limited supports The Forest Stewardship
Council (FSC), the leading international forest certification organisation.
All our titles that are printed on Greenpeace approved FSC certified paper
carry the FSC logo. Our paper procurement policy can be found at:
www.rbooks.co.uk/environment

Printed and bound in Great Britain by
CPI Cox & Wyman, Reading, RG1 8EX

For my mum and dad
Dolly and Tom
who have made so many of my memories
worth remembering

Contents

Preface

'Pull no more bines' was the call that echoed round the hop gardens, signalling the end of the day's work in the fields. Bines are the rough, vine-like stems of the hop plant, which have been grown in this country since Roman times. Hops were first grown as a vegetable and then for their more familiar use in beer making.

The cry of 'pull no more bines' was directed to the pole pullers, whose job was to cut the stringing which supported the growing plants. This released the bines which they then pulled down for the pickers to 'clean'. The pickers were mainly female workers, whose job was to strip the hop cones from the stems into big hessian containers supported on trestles – the hop bins. The hops were collected by the measurers then taken to the oast houses for drying. 'Pull no more bines' told the male pole pullers that their work was finished, but the women pickers weren't so lucky, they still had their domestic chores to attend to.

At the end of the day's picking the women returned to the hoppers' huts, their temporary homes during the harvest. There they would light the faggot fires on which they cooked their meals and did the washing up and laundry. Finally they could spend a while talking and laughing with the other women, sitting around the faggot fires, relaxing until they were more than ready for bed.

'Pull no more bines' is no longer called across the hop gardens of Kent. The fields now reverberate with the endless drone of machinery. Going to Kent in September is just a memory for the many thousands of women who, like me, my mother and my grandmothers before me, went down hopping.

Acknowledgments

I have to thank the many people who helped me complete this book, especially the women who allowed me to record their memories and stories.

Thank you to Richard Stutely at the Maidstone Museum, to Val Gibbons and her cousin Rita Game. Thank you also to listeners of the *Pete Murray Show* on London Talkback Radio who wrote and telephoned, particularly Mrs Blanchard and Miss Duckworth.

I am grateful for permission to quote from the following: *Swimming to Cambodia* by Spalding Grey (Picador); *Hopping Down in Kent* by Alan Bignell (Robert Hale); *Old Days in the Kent Hop Gardens* ed. Mary Lewis (West Kent Federation of Women's Institutes); *The Voice of the Past: Oral History* by Paul Thompson (Oxford University Press); *Home, Work and Class Consciousness* by Marilyn Porter (Manchester University Press); *Making Histories: Studies in History-writing and Politics*, the Centre of Contemporary Cultural Studies (Hutchinson Educational); 'The Peculiarities of Oral History' by Alessandro Portelli in *History Workshop Journal* 12 (Ruskin College Oxford); Simon Jenkins in the *Sunday Times*, 8 January 1989; the Women's History Issue of the *Journal of Oral History* (University of Essex).

The photographs are reproduced by kind permission of the Hulton Picture Company; Maidstone Museum; Museum of Kent Rural Life; and Rita Game. Other photographs are from the author's own collection.

Thank you to Lorraine Gamman for all her time and friendship.

The author apologises for any error or omissions in the above list. While all efforts have been made to trace the holders of copyright, this has not been possible in the case of some of the older texts. She would appreciate being notified of any corrections or additions.

Introduction: Memories and Stories

Well, that's a good story, but is it the truth? . . . Oh hell no, Howard, you know the Truth's no story t'all.
Spalding Gray[1]

If we'd known they were the good old days we might have enjoyed them more. Frances Clark[2]

It's only true. Mrs S[3]

I'm sitting in a big hessian bag, a hop bin, surrounded by tangles of dew-soaked bines. I'm stripping hops from the prickly stems. The sides of the bin go higher than the top of my head. It's early on what (I now know) must be an autumn morning. There are smells that are all mixed up: damp earth, wet sacking, tea stewing over the faggot fire near the hop bin. But stronger than all these is the overwhelming smell of hops. An odd smell, bitter and sickly sweet at the same time.

My roof is made of hop bines growing up and across the strings that link the chestnut poles – the bines that the pole puller hasn't cut down yet. Through the leaves the sky is blue and bright. My mum is laughing, talking with the other women.

I have other memories of 'going down hopping': chasing my cousin Jill around the huts, making her scream, even though she was much bigger than me, by biting lumps off a live worm. My brother Tony stealing a piglet and trying to hide it from Mum – the squealing gave him away. More glamorously, Tony being picked to appear in a film! A proper one that was shown at the cinema. I say to myself that it was because he had red hair, but the film would probably have been in black and white. Wouldn't it? Perhaps I wasn't even born. Perhaps they are not all memories but stories that my family, like families are meant to, tell and embroider and retell and laugh about. I know that I was there in the bin, and I know I ate the worm. I also know that it was me who tipped the newts into the bed, so that they wouldn't get cold. I was the one who was 'daft about animals' (excluding worms, I suppose).

My mother's memories about the same events can be different from mine. This confuses us and we sometimes disagree about 'what really happened'. Perhaps it's like the children's game of Chinese whispers. When you whisper to me, I don't hear what you say, but I hear what I know. Familiar words that make sense in my world, not yours.

It's easy to take other people's stories for granted, to undervalue them, when you think they'll always be there. They can tell the end of the story another day. The shock of loss is more acute when they're not around any more and you can't recall how a bit of the story goes. I think about trying to tell my children a story that their great grandmother told me: how she and her mother, on their way home from work at the music hall had seen the 'old boy'. The 'old boy' was a name for Jack the Ripper used by the girls and women who worked around the theatres and music halls of Whitechapel. It was a frightening story, but funny too, the way my nan told it. Sometimes she would sing a Marie Lloyd song she remembered.

The subtleties and details were, as in any translation, lost as I retold the story to my children. It was no longer the memories of a young girl in the Victorian East End of London, but a story, altered and reshaped by the memories and experiences of more recent times. The Ripper industry of the late 1980s contributed additional connotations and meanings to the tale.

It is not only widely known stories, such as those about the Whitechapel murders, which are embroidered or altered by retelling. I was told the following story about a hop picker's gravestone:

An old lady had been going to Kent for the hop harvest since she was a baby. All her life hopping had marked the coming of autumn, the time when the women and children made their annual journey to Kent. They would earn a bit of money and have a break from the slums of the East End. Hopping was important to many London women just like her, but for some reason it had held a special place in her life. Her happiest times had been spent in the hop gardens. When she died her headstone was engraved with the epitaph: 'PULL NO MORE BINES'. She had finished her labours for ever, and now she could rest in peace.

When I was collecting the oral testimonies, which make up the main part of this book, several women told me the story about the gravestone. They all understood the meaning of the story and its significance in their lives. It was a story about a time they remembered, with affection and laughter, and it had passed. Hop picking, like the old woman, had become history. They were moved as they told the story. Small details of the narrative varied, but they all related the tale with the conviction of people who knew they were speaking the truth. I tried to find the grave where the old woman had been buried, but failed. She was as elusive as a figure in a dream, a memory that is just out of focus, there but not quite within reach.

It doesn't matter whether or not the story is true. What matters is that the *idea* of the woman and her headstone touched something in the women who told the story. In their retelling the women took the opportunity to talk about loss, change and the continuation of things which they valued. The epitaph was a representation of their feelings, a powerful metaphor with a meaning that could be shared with others who knew about 'going down hopping'.

All the women who spoke to me about their experiences of the past wanted to have *their* stories remembered, they knew that it was important not to forget, nor to be forgotten. They wanted their past to be told in ways that they would recognise.

G: All these stories you've told me. They'd have been lost if you hadn't been kind enough to see me. Not lost really. Not shared, is what I mean. Perhaps that's the same.

Mrs B: That's right. I think that. I hope that you *can* put it in a book.

Mrs AB: They was lovely times and they shouldn't be forgotten . . . I like a good book.

Mrs B: I'll ask my daughter. She's got a couple of hardback books through her bookclub. You can see them. But they're not our stories. They don't tell them like us.

G: It's funny. I was saying that to my mum. Telling things different ways. When she tells me about hopping it's not how I remember it. Some of it is. But some things are really different. She says it's because I was little, and I'm remembering that. Being little.

Mrs AB: Yeh, when you went, you was a kid. You didn't have to graft, like your mum. All you remember was being on your holidays![4]

Mrs AB made me think again about inconsistencies in people's recollections of the past. I thought about how we and our parents can remember the past so differently that we seem to be talking about totally unrelated events. But still we value and need the act of remembering.

Memory is part of a creative act which we work on the framework of our knowledge and experience of past events. The shape we arrive at is formulated (even dictated) by our present perspective and preoccupations, letting us understand more about ourselves and our place in the world.

We know that memories can be called upon or repressed, or, more alarmingly, can creep up and surprise us. Except in the cases of accident or disease our memories are always there, even when we have no immediate use for them. We are right to fear the amnesia that can come with old age; it means the loss of identity.

I once lost a part of my identity, the part of me that had been hop picking. I didn't actually lose my memory, but suppressed it for a while; it didn't seem necessary to acknowledge that bit of myself. I did not identify with those particular memories because another framework was being fitted around me, by other people. Memories about hop picking had no place in my new world. I was a girl who passed exams and who would be part of a different future.

New explanations about my identity were available, memories about hopping would have been out of place. I had passed the eleven plus, a scholarship girl, so I was bussed daily to the school where I had 'won' a place. The uniform, the signal of my achievements (and therefore of my friends' failure), marked me out. I was a target. I could be ignored, scorned, even envied, but worst of all I was set apart. The bus journey home could be difficult. Despite the pressure, I lasted at the school, a place of opportunity and privilege, until I was 15. My answer to the conflict of not fitting in with the new world was to escape. The head teacher was angry that I was leaving before taking all those O levels, but wasn't really that surprised. I was confirming all the statistics. Working class girls had no educational staying power, the drop-out rates showed that clearly. No one questioned the reasons for the statistics in those days.

It was a long time before I realised that I *could* question what I felt were false assumptions about me. I could value my own explanations of the world, based on different understandings of what happened in my life. I no longer needed to wonder if my version of the past was proper 'History', or if it would be counted as the 'Truth'. It *would* be my version and it would make sense and have meaning for me. The feeling of getting things right, of things fitting, was what mattered. I found the comfort of completing a puzzle, the gaps being filled at last. But this was plastering over cracks in my identity. Things *don't* fit so easily, not unless the edges have been rubbed away and made smooth to make them neat. The nature of memory is the same as that of all other historical evidence: it is malleable. It can be selected and edited so that it will fit. Any writer can fill her literary trolley full of favourite ingredients then form them into the recipe that takes her fancy. It is crucial for both the writer and the reader to remember that books can be cooked.

Records of the past can bring much pleasure, but critical awareness should always be present, operating as a rubbish detector. Critical awareness highlights and questions both the form and content of the text, looking for the hidden agenda, camouflaged by seductively fascinating detail. Oral history, having a wealth of such detail, should make the reader particularly suspicious about the motives of the writer.

At the time when I started to think more carefully about the problems with the recording of oral history, I was invited to a history conference to talk about collecting the hop picking stories. I was disappointed when somebody asked me, in a genuinely concerned tone, how I could decide whether the women, who talked to me about their memories, were telling the 'Truth'. Next I was asked what I did if the women did not give 'politically sound' responses to my enquiries about their lives. The people who asked these questions believed (with a lack of analysis more appropriate to acts of religious faith than to the practice of history), that there is a single truth which can be revealed (presumably by a holy person who has been blessed with a politically sound attitude). Such attitudes can lead to some serious misunderstandings about what history is or can be, both as a cultural and commercial product.

We need our memories and, at a very basic level, we need a notion of personal history through which we understand our identities. We need to place what we know within a structure, which in turn enables us to make sense of our knowledge. But we also need formal histories to provide the wider structures in which we place our lives. The following section – 'A Brief History of Hop Picking in Kent' – provides such a structure, in which the reader can place the oral testimonies in this book.

A Brief History of Hop Picking in Kent

Harvesting has been done by hand since hops were first introduced into Britain by the Romans, although the young hop shoots were used in those days as a vegetable rather than for brewing.

Hops were grown in many parts of England, but it was the comparatively close Kent farms which attracted the London pickers. The annual trip to the hop gardens became a tradition in many families, sometimes with whole streets going to the same farm. By the late nineteenth century east Londoners had become the main source of casual labour employed by Kent farmers during the hop harvest.

Until the 1950s and 1960s, when machine picking became widespread, there were so few changes in methods of hop cultivation that the 1850 season would have been almost indistinguishable from that of 1950. The only major innovation, from the pickers' point of view, had been the introduction of 'stringing'. This was a method of training the plants up twine, tied between chestnut supports, rather than growing them up the poles themselves.

It has been estimated that while hand picking was still the main method of gathering the hops, between one hundred thousand and a quarter of a million people made the journey from London to go 'down hopping'. According to English Hops Ltd (the hop marketing co-operative) there are now just two farms in Kent which still employ Londoners to hand pick in the traditional way. During the research for this book I made several visits to one of these, a small enterprise which was making very little money from growing hops. However, as labour shortages increased and the demand for hops declined, the forces for change won. When I last visited the farm the plants had been grubbed up and the fields cleared. Hops were no longer being grown.

In the period with which the oral testimonies in this book are concerned, approximately 1920 to 1970, the majority of pickers were women. If they were 'foreigners' – the term used for Londoners and other non-local pickers – they would take their children and other dependent relatives to stay on the farm in the hoppers' huts. Adult male relatives would visit them at the weekends.

The local pickers were also usually female, but they were referred to, and considered themselves to be, 'home dwellers'.

The distinction between foreigners and home dwellers was more than nominal; it characterised the fear and distrust that often existed between the two groups.

This predominantly female, working class experience has all but disappeared as circumstances in the hop industry have changed – paralleled in many ways by other changes in the women's lives. Soon all manual harvesting will be at an end, and with it an important part of many people's lives.

It was about 30 years ago that hand picking as the chief method of harvesting began to be threatened seriously, when large numbers of machines were introduced into the west Midlands. Initially, this was in response to the acute labour shortage which was causing problems in most industries in the post-war years. At the same time, expectations about health standards were being raised, and public health officials were beginning to demand that hoppers' accommodation should be ventilated and have at least basic sanitary facilities. Machine harvesting was soon found to be more cost effective than employing large numbers of better-accommodated hand pickers. A precedent of machine efficiency had been set.

Machines were making an impact in other sections of the economy. The London women, who had traditionally made up the major part of Kent's casual labour force, were being presented with increasing opportunities for regular, paid work. This was mostly part-time, on the newly introduced twilight or housewives' shifts, in the manufacturing and processing industries.

Workers with full-time jobs began to expect, and to get, paid annual leave. A week or two at the seaside or in a holiday camp became an affordable possibility even for manual workers. For many cockney families, going to the caravan, or chalet, soon challenged going down hopping in popularity. With their new spending power and improved working conditions, many Londoners came to regard hopping as a pleasant break in the countryside rather than as a way of earning money.

The Kent hop farmers could no longer depend on the

availability of enough women workers at the right time. The pool of casual, seasonal labour was drying up. Even those pickers who still made the annual journey to Kent presented difficulties for their temporary employers. The increased expectations relating to pay and conditions were beginning to filter down from the full-time workers. This was probably more to do with the new affluence of the post-war boom and the bargaining power resulting from the labour shortages, than with any official action on health and safety.

Whatever the causes of the difficulties with labour, the effect was the same: the farmers realised that if their acreage was sufficient to warrant it, mechanisation was the solution to their post-war problems.

A more recent threat has caused concern throughout the English hop industry, one that is as serious as the wilt disease had been before the introduction of disease free strains. Changing British taste has meant that the drinks market has moved to lager and wine, and to strong 'imported' beers. This has resulted in a declining demand for the types of hop which, traditionally, have been grown in Kent. Many of the popular German-type beers are brewed in Britain under licence, on the understanding that only female hops are used. Ironically, the high fertility of the Kent soil makes the cultivation of female-only hop plants almost impossible. According to a variety of sources from the Brewers' Society to individual growers, the rich soil has enabled wild male hops to flourish. These 'rampant weeds' then find their way into the hop gardens, fertilise the female plants and make the crop useless for brewing the German-type product.

The problems resulting from the changing market have been exacerbated by the EC 'hop mountain', which in turn has been compounded by the availability of cheap Yugoslavian and American produced hops. The market is, of course, demand led, and when even machine harvesting cannot guarantee a profit, more Kent farmers are grubbing up their hops each year, leaving their fields empty. Fewer east London women make the annual journey to the hop gardens, except perhaps to visit the

Museum of Kent Rural Life at Maidstone, where they can see the work they once did reconstructed as part of the theme park world of 'rustic' England: hop picking without the mud but also without the people.

This book presents itself to the reader as a chronicle of some of the stories and the laughter of those people who went hopping, including my family. It is a combination of personal memory and oral testimony. One of the photographs shows my mum, a neighbour's daughter and me standing by a hop bin – I'm the one with the plaits. It is also a celebration of working class lives and experiences, told by women who are too often ignored, forgotten or, worse, who have been misrepresented by traditional histories.

The women whose memories appear in the oral testimonies are identified by initials only. This was done as a matter of courtesy as they were assured of confidentiality when they spoke to me about their often difficult lives. Brief, anonymous, biographical details of the women are included at the end of the book.

Part Two is a consideration of some of the ethical and theoretical issues surrounding the uses and abuses of oral history. From an academic viewpoint, I felt that it was vital to try to treat both the process of collecting the testimonies and the final product, the book, as honestly as I could. I wanted to consider the difficulties of representing other people's words within a structure that I was creating: to highlight the artificiality of translating the spoken word to the written page; to say how hard it was to deal with views that were sometimes at complete odds with my own; and to acknowledge all the other problems of having living women as both the subjects and object of a book. I wanted to avoid what has become the orthodox approach of oral historians which, to me, seems to use people's testimonies as just another source of usable material. I have tried, in Chapter 12, to consider an alternative use of evidence.

If I was to do justice to the women who gave me their time and showed me such kindness, then integrity in handling the 'raw material', their lives, was paramount. It was, therefore, a deliberate decision to leave these theoretical considerations to the end. The oral testimonies are the point of the book and these can be read as a history in themselves; they stand alone without further comment if the reader chooses to use the book in that way.

I believe that memories and stories have an importance in our lives that most of us understand. We don't usually theorise this understanding but we experience it often: when we were small we would ask to hear about 'the old days', or we would say, 'tell me about when I was little'. Our memories, our histories, give us a way of thinking about ourselves, our lives and our losses. This book translates those thoughts into words. I hope that you enjoy reading them as much as I enjoyed the privilege of meeting the women, collecting their stories, writing and remembering.

Notes

1 Gray, Spalding, *Swimming to Cambodia*, Picador, London, 1987, p. 261.
2 Clark, Frances, 'You Mean there are Still Real Cowboys?' BBC 2 television documentary, quoted in the *Guardian*, 6 September 1987.
3 Mrs S quoted in Chapter 2, p. 34.
4 Attribution of interview extracts: if the quote is from a discussion between two or more people, the speakers' initials are given at the beginning of each part of their conversation. If the extract is from one person's speech only, then their initials are given after the quote.

Part 1

1
The Women and Why they Picked

'You didn't see a lot of wildlife in Canning Town.'

The things that stand out was the company and the enjoy-
ment on the field. The atmosphere on the field was always
happy. There never seemed to be misery. There was always a
happy atmosphere there. I thought it was good. You got
away from London, had a breath of fresh air for the children,
built them up. You got a bit of money at the end. We sort of
saved up before we went. We got our food ready, our tins of
food. And it didn't really cost us a lot. But what money we
earned hop picking, we might come home with a bit! *Mrs M*

There is no single reason why so many London women went to
Kent as casual agricultural labourers during the hop harvest.
There is no single answer to why they were prepared to suffer
the hardships and deprivations of living in hoppers' huts. As
Mrs M begins to explain above, the reasons were varied,
overlapping and often contradictory. This first chapter looks at
some of the reasons the women *themselves* give for why they
went hopping. But as will be seen later, the reasons for the
yearly migration to Kent changed, as did the hop harvest, the
women and their lives.

Whether the women saw picking as a holiday or as paid work
depended partly on their financial circumstances, but also on
their skill and speed as pickers. The following comment was

made by Mrs D, a woman who saw hopping as part of the yearly cycle of agricultural work to which she and her family were tied:

> You see now, I'd go hopping, do a bit of fruiting. Time I'd done hopping and one thing and another – I could pick hops – so that I'd come home with a nice few bob saved up for Christmas. That's how I used to do it . . . I used to pick 60 bushels of hops a day, on my own, see? . . . I always had a bin on my own. There you are, that's my old hopping book there. That's how many hops I used to pick! Sixty, sixty-four a day. I was good at it . . . I was very quick. Good with my hands. *Mrs D*

Mrs D was a fast picker, exceptional in fact, and as a representative of English Hops Ltd agreed, it was not sensible to go hopping for 'big money' unless you had such skill.

The need for money to buy special things for Christmas, finding extra shillings for specific items like winter coats, or simply to meet a surprisingly big bill, were all mentioned by women as being important reasons for going hopping. What might be considered luxuries at other times of the year could effectively become necessities at Christmas time.

> *Mrs S*: I used to put the hopping money away for Christmas for the kids' toys and new clothes and that.

> *Mrs C*: When we were kids that's what my mum used to do. It would clear her debts and loans . . .

> *Mrs S*: Money for the tally man! Like old whatsisname down Burdett Road.

> *Mrs ML*: That was the only way I got my school uniform, Mum picking hops.

> *Mrs C*: And we'd all have a new velvet dress, Christmas – out of the hopping money. 'You don't pick,' she'd say, 'and you don't get no new dress.' You had to work like bloody hell to get that velvet dress.

Not all the women who went hopping specifically to earn money did so to pay for extras, or because their skill made it worthwhile. Some women went because they had little choice or opportunity of finding alternative waged work.

Mrs AA used to go to Kent with her grandmother, aunts and cousins:

My family had to pick for the money. They were poor. They'd have to make the kids pick. My nan needed the money. There was 13 kids in the family . . . She obviously went for the money, but it was a break as well from life in London. But the money came first. It was a way of earning a wage with all the kids. I don't think she could have done that in London. See there was so many kids. What work could you do with all them around you? You could work, see, *and* keep an eye on us. And everybody, all of us, earned our own little bits . . . see, me nan went primarily for the money. She had to. Me grandad drank most of his money away. It was hard work for me nan. She'd have a laugh but it was hard work. She used to have to earn her money. It was different for other women and kids. But see even though it was hard graft and she needed the money, it was her break. It meant a real lot to her. She got knocked around by me grandad – drink again, it's always drinking. We used to see a lot of it. So getting away down hopping was something to look forward to. It was a break away from him. It was a different way of life.

The significance of hopping being a job where the women could take their children is looked at in more detail later in the book. But it wasn't just 'childcare provision' that mattered to the women, they also acknowledged how important it was that the elderly, the less able, very young babies and even household pets, could all be taken hopping. Most of the women remembered this as a particular perk, which helped to make their lives easier. Mrs C (who cleaned the Mansion House steps on her knees every week-day morning and two evenings, using just soapy water and a scrubbing brush), pointed out that in London many of the women found it necessary but hard to leave their children at home, often still asleep, while they went out to work.

> You could have your children with you down hopping. Not like the cleaning work I had in London . . . That was hard. *Mrs C*

> All of us went. Nan, kids, aunts, cousins. We used to take the horse. We even took the goldfinches in their cage! *Mrs D*

It was not only the relief, and convenience, of being able to keep her child with her that Mrs M remembered. Hopping was also a 'treat'. She and her in-laws went because:

> That was their summer holiday . . . I used to go when Aunt F was down there . . . I used to look forward to the holiday.

Mrs S, on the other hand, thought that *her* in-laws emphasised the holiday aspect of hopping to show that they did not have to go for the money.

> They thought they were a bit posh. They used to make a fuss about it being a holiday – to prove they were comfortable! It was no good *us* pretending. Our mum had to do it for the money. *Mrs S*

Earning some money to take home at the end of the season did not seem to be an issue for some of the pickers. For instance, Mrs J, who used to go hopping as a girl, and now has the tenancy of a pub next to a hop farm, made the following observation about some of her hopping customers:

> I don't know how they earned any money out of it, all the money they earnt was all spent on beer anyway!

Mrs RR's aunt was a business woman who 'had money', but

still went hopping for her holidays even though she could have afforded something different.

My old Aunt H had money. She owned a florist in the old market and still always used to go hopping. Still went. She had a few bob. My mum used to work for her. That good business and she still went hopping . . . definitely didn't go hopping for the money. I mean, even the jewellery she left. You know it was only in the latter years that she bothered to go abroad . . . it was always hopping . . . go down there for a month or more and come home every Wednesday to have a sauna down the East Ham baths!

Mrs RR's aunt had another reason for going hopping, one that she shared with other women I spoke to. For Aunt H, hopping wasn't just a holiday, it was also a legitimate reason to be away from her husband.

See for years my Aunt H and Uncle C, well, they never got on. And, er, I think, er, he had another woman. You know . . . It wasn't very good, all that. *Mrs RR*

Mrs AA's grandmother had similar problems.

I love my nan. I can sit and listen to her stories for ever. I get choked . . . See even though it was hard graft and she needed the money, it was her break. It meant a real lot to her. She got knocked round a bit by my grandad. Drink again. It's always drinking. We used to see a lot of it. [Pause] So, getting away down hopping was something to look forward to. It was a break away from *him* to a different way of life. The mud puddles with your wellies. Mostly nice weather! Few wet days when all the water'd run up your arms from the bines. But you imagine, in the pissing down – oops! – the *pouring* down of rain [laughter] and someone starts a conversation, or a song. Imagine it! Kids all in the mud with their wellies.

Wouldn't have to worry. [Pause] 'Roll Out the Barrel.' And all that!

Even the women who had no money to spare, and who might have to find some extra cash to go hopping, would still be glad to get to Kent for the harvest.

G: Was it the holiday or the money that was important?

Mrs C: Holiday. Because you couldn't afford a holiday, otherwise. Don't know about you.

Mrs S: We never had no holiday, never. Apart from hopping.

Mrs C: That was ours. That was ours.

Mrs ML: We used to ask, 'What's for dinner?', and Mum'd [Mrs C] say, 'I'll see what I can afford.' And we had something, but holiday . . . Only holiday we ever had.

G: So, could you earn?

Mrs C: No, not there. Not there. [The particular farm that they went to.] Well, I never did, and my mother never did, because it was a working farm where you had to pick so many hops. You know, to earn sort of, well, you couldn't even earn a pound a day. And, er, well I think to myself: it was a *hard way of living*, for what you earned for what you done. And the hours you put at it. Yes!

G: Could you earn more at home, in London?

Mrs C: Yes, but here you'd have your holiday, and your children with you. Actually you was taking a cut in your money. It cost you more to live down there – you know it do . . . But, of course, you've still got to remember the rate of money then. See? I had to save up to come down hopping.

G: You had to save up to go hopping?

Mrs C: Yes. But in London. I'll tell you the truth. I did cleaning in the Mansion House. Twenty-five bob a week *and* go back twice a week on an evening. Know what I used to do in the Mansion House? Clean them *bloody steps* outside. That was my job. Yes.

G: You didn't? With little ones. What hard work. What times did you have to do?

Mrs C: Six. Our time was six in the morning till nine. Then twice a week we used to go back. Twenty-five shillings for that.

G: Hopping must've seemed a doddle!

If women like Mrs A's grandmother were getting away from drunken men – for the hop harvest at least (see above and Chapter 6) – others, like Mrs C, were getting away from the hardships of city life. With the development of modern transport systems and the increase in private car ownership, the hop gardens now seem much nearer to east London, but during the war years they could have been in another world. This was particularly true in those years when the East End was being bombarded during the blitz. By going to Kent the women and their children could escape the horrors of the air raids which affected so many London families, killing loved ones and destroying their homes. Later, when the war was over, they could temporarily escape the housing shortage which, for many of them, meant living in cramped, sub-standard conditions, billeted on neighbours or family. Mrs M talked about many benefits of living the country life.

It was different hours, different environment. You got away from it – London. You got away from that being 'cramped in' in London. Once you got out in the fields it was so different. When you was in London you was squashed in. That's how it seems to me. People. You was all free down hopping. Relaxed. If you went to Southend you was lucky. Even when we went to Loughton for the day, from the mission, that was wonderful. This was further away, and we stayed there! It was beautiful . . . During the war, especially, we decided to go down to get away from London, if you know what I mean . . . that's when we took R [her daughter]. It was Mr M's family what actually *did* it [the picking]. I went for the break. To get away from the raids.

The Kent countryside did not escape the bombs entirely. Mr D, a hop farmer, provided a rural version of the air raid shelter for the pickers.

Mr D: We had a plane come down here! We had one crash in the hop garden when we was picking! That caused a scene. The bloke who crashed in the hop garden, by the time we got him out, was dead. That was a Messerschmitt 109. We had a big dyke dug up there – soon as the warnings went they used to stand down in it. Below ground. And when the all clear went they'd go back out on the bins.

G: Did you have much trouble round here?

Mr D: See, we had the worst day. About eight raids that day.

G: Not so bad as London with the blitz then?

Mr D: Oh yeh! I mean the only time they dropped their bombs here was when they got shot or tried to get back. Otherwise they'd carry on to London, obviously. See?

It was not just violent men – whether husbands or bombers – that the women were glad to leave behind. Many of the women's recollections were from the days before smokeless zones were introduced, making the contrast between the Kent countryside and inner London even more vivid. Going hopping was as much about the desire to leave the choking atmosphere of the polluted city (if only for a while) as it was about the draw of working in the greenery of the hop fields, even if the source of the greenery was sometimes a little surprising for town dwellers.

Mrs T: You know how you used to walk through the fields after you'd finished picking one? You'd have to move through that field to the next one. I'll *never* forget one morning when I got up. I'd never experienced anything like it. There was all these people walking across to the next field and I like saw these, a big line of green things. All hopping! And I said, 'Whatever's that?' And they said they was grasshoppers. Well. Like, as the people were walking through the fields, they was moving. I'll never forget that. Like a long line, moving. You didn't see a lot of wildlife in Canning Town!

Mrs R: No, the birds never sang there – they coughed!

It wasn't just the birds in Canning Town, the children coughed too. Their mothers looked on the fresh air of the Kent countryside as an important boost to the children's health. Their offspring could be 'built up' and have their lungs 'unclogged' to make them strong enough to withstand the coming winter that brought seasonal ill health and increased child mortality. Kent County Council (KCC), however, were more concerned with the children's possible ill health in the summer. Medical care and other support services for the yearly influx of Londoners meant bigger bills. Instead of seeing the hoppers as the vital source of casual labour which the farmers knew them to be, the local authority viewed the hoppers as potential sources of epidemics and users of costly services – a threatening 'other' to upset the tranquillity and order of the rural idyll.

Arguments between the Kent and London county councils began and continued. Finally, Kent demanded that the LCC contribute to any additional costs incurred as a result of the Londoners' presence. The debate was particularly bitter about provision for the hoppers' children. The KCC claimed that the children were of no economic value and did not contribute to the harvest, but were in Kent's beautiful countryside for the sake of their health. (This was not that far from the truth in many cases.) London made the counter argument that the women and children would not be there at all had their labour not been needed so badly by the Kent hop growers.

Whether it was the hoppers or the farmers who were the real 'winners' was an official argument, conducted at the level of conferences and public reports, between the county councils. Superficially, at least, the women's experiences and memories seem to support Kent's belief that it was the Londoners who came out best. Mrs AB told the following story:

Pound and half born! I must've been like a bleeding rabbit, mustn't I? And my mum said hopping was the making of me. I was born in the April, see, and I wasn't getting on very well. I was born indoors. And one of the neighbours – Aunt Ginny as we used to call her, another adopted aunt! – said to my mum, 'Bring her down hopping.' She'd been down hopping for years, you see. And my mum said, 'No, it'll kill her.' My mum hadn't been before. She said, 'Course it won't. You bring her down.' So mum took me and the three youngest boys. Aunt Ginny wrote to the farmer and said she wanted another bin, was it all right? And they wrote back and said yes it was, so we had a hut for ourselves and a bin. And as I say when we went back I was twice the size I'd been before I went. Four and half pounds when I went back from hopping. Born a pound and half. And I went every year after that. And whatever job I had, my mum used to make me pack it up. Yeh, to come hopping, 'cos she said it was the making of me. Well a lot of them used to come just to earn money, but a lot of them didn't. My mum used to come 'cos she said it built you up for the winter. All the bad fogs you got in London, the kids'd get chesty and that.

Yet KCC appear to have deliberately understated the importance of the vast numbers of pickers required each year for the harvest. As the LCC pointed out, without the Londoners, there would have been no harvest. They also reinforced the point made by Mrs AB above, that many gave up their regular jobs to do casual work in the hop fields. Farmer D's memories could be used to support either side of the argument.

I mean, they used to come away and they'd have to give their jobs up. Otherwise the children never got out of London at all, did they? They used to come down here and it'd be three or four days before they finished choking, time they'd got all the soot off their lungs. And them days, course, when they used to get the smogs and fogs. I been up there and when you blow your nose, it's black . . . people'd be walking around with scarves round their faces . . . you don't hear of fogs in London now . . . But those days they used to be. Well a lot of the pickers used to come down Easter and wouldn't go back till after hop picking. Stay right through the season. Strawberry picking, currant picking, whatever there was going.

The local authorities had concerns other than the health – or lack of it – of the pickers' children. They were also concerned with their school attendance – or lack of it. How the pickers viewed the annual break in their, or their children's, education depended on their view of the schools and the relative importance to them of going hopping. Mrs A, one of the younger informants, had strong views on missing school.

I think in the London schools they used to take it for granted. I think so, you know. It was the done thing for so many kids anyway. Mind you I was never really at school anyway. Always used to have the truant officer round! I was always on the hop! Wonder if that's where it comes from? 'On the hop' 'cos of going down hopping? As a kid then I'd really look forward to getting away down to hopping.

The idea that missing school did not matter too much if you were a Londoner was also held by Mrs D who missed school every year. When she became a mother her own children did the same, and it was her turn to take them, as their grandmother had taken her.

Mrs D: They never used to take no notice then. Everybody did it then, didn't they? I should think schools could have shut up when it was hopping time. Round our way.

G: How about the local school board man? Did he used to go to the fields looking for the local Kent kids?

Mrs D: That's right, yeh. He was always looking for them. But no one used to take no notice of us, did they, coming from London. Our mum and dad had us all ready on the Monday we went home. We was all washed and polished. Take a note to tell 'em you'd been hopping. And er, just go back in school. And we used to stop there *all* winter, you know. Yeh, we used to go to school regular, every winter. Never in the summer.

Sending in a 'note' was quite usual but not all the notes explained where the children had actually been.

Mrs C: I'd send a letter in. That was it. They'd gone on their annual holiday. I never said 'hop picking'. Annual holiday.

Mrs M: Lot of them said, 'We're going down the chalet!' Not hopping.

Mrs C: Yeh. Not the hop hut. [Mock posh voice] 'The chalet.'

Mrs T's mother didn't have the opportunity to send her note. The 'school board man' came to the house while her daughter was away hopping with a friend's family.

My mother said to the school board man when he came, 'Oh! she's gone away with her auntie to Ilfracombe in Devon.' And he said, 'What a lucky little girl!' [Laughing] I never even seen Devon! I'd never even been down Southend, let alone Devon.

Other women didn't see any point in making excuses; their

families had little choice about going hopping. As Mrs AB explained:

> We used tell 'em they'd be away. Wasn't much they could do. There were so many kids would be away. Most of the really poor kids had to go. For the money, for their health and that. No, the schools couldn't do nothing, could they?

Farmer D, as an employer of hop pickers, was affected only marginally by the children missing their education.

> Well, in them days, it was no problem. But after the war, like now, if they want to come down here they just report. And you know I have no bother. We used to have forms at one time. The farmers would have to sign it and they was all right – to say the family was working hop picking. Oh special forms we used to sign.

Whether the children would have missed even more school due to ill health is something which can only be guessed at. What is certain is that going hopping was too important in their lives for a little thing like the school board to stop them. Their feelings about the work and what the experience meant to the hoppers were puzzled over by Mrs R and Mrs T.

> *Mrs R*: It was just a thing you did. It was more a holiday than anything else for us. Never had a holiday, did we? Well we never did . . .

> *Mrs T*: We was exploited really. All for a pittance we earned, didn't we?

> *Mrs R*: And when you think about our conditions! We *was* exploited . . . and it rained solid for a fortnight . . . well after a fortnight they'd had enough. Couldn't pick, couldn't do nothing. And that's all they'd gone down there for wasn't it? . . . A bit of bun money wasn't it? [Money for luxuries] . . . They used to have to work hard, and not for that much.

When they tallied at the end of each day [worked out the day's earnings], you'd never get that much down on your card. Plenty of them had nothing to start with. They'd have a sub almost as soon as they got down there . . . But then I think we really enjoyed it. I did. I did enjoy it.

Mrs T: But when you think of it these days. It was a working holiday, wasn't it? It wasn't much of holiday for adults really I suppose. But it was for the younger ones.

Mrs R: I don't know the reasons they still go [her cousins who still work on a mechanised farm]. They don't need the money. My C still goes down to them for weekends. It's just like having a chalet I suppose. See it's what you've always classed as your holiday. Even though sometimes it was a bit rough, it was your holiday.

And as Mrs AA said:

I don't know how they even knew [about particular farms] but I suppose it was in the family before them. It's always been there. Like me, I first got to know of it 'cos I was always taken. To me it was the expected thing, at a certain time of the year, to go hopping.

2
Preparations and Journeys

'Have you got your letter yet?'

'Have you got your letter yet?' was a question asked by, and of, women throughout working class London from the nineteenth century onwards. Getting 'your letter' was the sign that you had been accepted by 'your' farmer for another year's harvesting. As well as confirming your employment and accommodation it would give the date when picking would begin. On rare occasions regulars would not receive a letter – a sign that they had, in some way, antagonised their temporary employer during the previous season. Perhaps they had stolen something more than the acceptable few apples from the orchards. Perhaps they had not 'behaved' after drinking in the village. Whatever the reason, they had been barred.

The tradition of the letter developed from the nineteenth century practice of London-based agents providing letters of recommendation – references – for prospective pickers to show the hop growers. This system operated as a means of controlling which and how many Londoners would 'invade' the Kent countryside. The threat of the existence of an unruly horde has always been present in the popular imagination. Cockney invaders were a particularly potent version of the myth. The letter as a licence to pick survived the far shorter-lived agencies.

And the excitement of waiting for that hopping letter! Used to go up and down the road, didn't it? Course it was the same families who went every year wasn't it? *Mrs RR*

There was genuine pride in being the 'right sort' of family – the sort of family who received their letter, demonstrating that they had been selected as suitable. Once the letter arrived the preparations for the sojourn in the country could begin in earnest. These arrangements were considerable, as provision had to be made for staying away from home for as long as eight weeks. The length of the stay depended on the co-operation of the weather, the variety of hops and whether the pickers were employed to help with the fruit harvest.

Some women (like Mrs C) were granted the privilege of not having to take all their household needs and equipment with them every year. These were regulars particularly favoured by the farmers and were allowed to leave large items in their 'own' huts. Dressers with displays of china, washstands, wardrobes, babies' cots, tables and chairs could all be stored for the next year.

We even had a bed. A proper bed spring. Raised on the big base end at first, but eventually we brought our own springs and rested them on apple boxes to pull them off the floor. And that was our bed. We was allowed to leave them there. *Mrs C*

Even for those accorded this favour there was still a great deal to be transported from London to the hop fields. In the days when private transport was rare, if not unheard of, in working class communities, this must have been a momentous task. The women would collect anything they could, packing everything from clothing to teaspoons, bags of sugar to bed ticking, and all the nappies necessary in those 'greener', if less convenient, pre-disposable days. Everything available would be amassed in amounts to last through the season. This even included the boys' haircuts.

The mums would take their kids for a tuppenny all off. A hopping haircut. The barber would shave their hair right up the back and just leave a bit at the front. Like a fringe. That'd last right till the end of hopping. *Mrs S*

Apart from the boys and their haircuts everything else to be taken to Kent went into the hopping box. The hopping box was both a central and a useful feature of the preparations. It served as a year-round reminder of the countryside (each time that an item was identified as being of future use, mothers throughout London would say: 'Put that in the hopping box!'), and a mobile container for easier transportation of all the goods. The box itself was frequently an ingenious example of recycling. Often not a box at all but more usually a converted pram with a tea chest or other stout container strapped on to the wheels.

We had a hopping box on four wheels . . . We took our hopping box, a sack, a load of parcels, old clothes . . . water buckets. We had no running water. So really it was all your usual domestic things that you had to take. *Mrs C*

'That's all right for down hopping – stick it in the box!' Mum'd say. *Mrs S*

Many of the women were from very poor families who had little that wasn't old or secondhand, but they would still put away their very oldest possessions for use 'down hopping'.

Mrs T: I used to go with a friend of mine, and her mother used to have an old crate, a big thing. And they used to put all these old things in there. All their cast offs. Then the old table would come out. The old chairs. Used to give them all a scrub. All the old gear in the house used to go. Old pots and pans, knives and forks. The old bassinet.

Mrs RR: Used to take all the old ticks, didn't we?

Mrs T: What you'd call now the 'duvet covers'! Stuff that with straw. Take all the old lace curtains . . . Used to take ornaments even. All to make the huts look better. Even wallpaper.

Mrs AB's family were less formal in their storage arrangements:

All year round, if we had anything, someone'd say, 'We don't want this any more.' And she'd (her mother) say . . . 'Put it under the bed. Put it under the bed. It'll do for hopping.'

The only things that might be made especially for hop picking were the hoppers' aprons.

Mrs D: Big aprons. Mother used to make the aprons. If she had a bit of stuff in the middle of the year she'd make all the aprons. Yeh. Used to make us all big black aprons. With big pockets.

G: My nan always used to wear them. Hers were big cross-over ones.

Mrs D: My mum's were big black ones with horseshoe pockets. I've still got her last one upstairs. There'd always be something in there. Something for us. She'd be diving around in the big pockets!

Preparations over, the day of the journey came at last. The methods of transport, like the means of storage, varied according to what the women could afford or what was available locally.

G: Did they [Green Line buses] go all the way?

Mrs AB: No. Just to Tunbridge Wells then change . . . You know some of them used to walk, even with little ones. That was even cheaper than the trains. And you could fiddle them. And some had their old wagons. The farmers had their wagons and they used to pick them up at the station to take them down the farm.

It is remarkable that some women recall making the whole journey on foot, even when they were very young children. Walking from London to the Kent countryside, to earn their hopping money:

. . . we used to walk every step of the way from here (east London) to Yalding, we did. Yeh, we used to catch the first ferry from Woolwich. Five o'clock. With the horse . . . we'd get off the ferry and walk there. Get there in the late afternoon. Mum'd have time to get all the beds ready and our tea cooked before it got dark. Before we lit the lamp. And we used to walk every step of the way. I've seen Mum carry a ten-day-old baby all the way. With the horse and cart with all the gear on it. And we just used to wander along. *Mrs D*

Many families found it possible to travel by train only because, as Mrs AB pointed out, it was easy to 'fiddle' the fares. Many women did. The stories vary as to how the fare dodging was accomplished but the two following examples include most of the features common to the tricks described by other informants (including popular stories often retold in my family):

We'd get off at the station from London, and he'd say 'Tickets!' And we'd say, 'She's got them!' And you'd be going through. You'd all be out the gate, wouldn't you, gone before they got you [lot of laughter]. Through the gate before the last one come through with *one* ticket. The ones that came down hopping on the trains used to tell stories! They'd put the kids under the seats, up on the racks . . . Once we brought the hopping box on the train from London Bridge. Got the train at three in the morning. Used to get up at ten o'clock at night. And it was: 'Get under the seat, you!' [pointing at her daughter] So you didn't have to pay. *Mrs C*

Mrs ML: Under the seats. All the kids had to go down there.

Mrs S: That's it. None of them'd pay. Hide under Mum's big coat.

Mrs C: The fare was three shillings.

Mrs ML: Tell Nan when you'd want to do a wee and she'd lift the lid up off the hopping box and get the piss pot out.

Mrs C: (laughing) Oi! You could have said 'poss pit'.

Mrs S: It's only true.

Contemporary photographs show enormous crowds of Londoners waiting for the 'Hoppers' Specials'. These were the trains, laid on at special cheap rates, which took the pickers in the early hours from the bedlam of the overcrowded platforms of London Bridge to the peace of the Kent countryside.

For some of the adults it was a worrying time; they were going 'on spec', trying their luck alongside their friends and neighbours who had been guaranteed paid work and accommodation. They would gather with the rest of the crowds, hours before the trains were due, to ensure a place – for the journey at least.

For the children, however, the adventure had begun.

Mrs L: I can remember walking down in the dark. That was a great adventure. There was a trolley on wheels. Aunt F used to be dragging it, like a big old pram. And all my cousins walking along there.

Mrs M: All piled up with your blankets, pots and pans.

Mrs L: I can remember walking down the street in the dark . . .

Mrs M: We went to London Bridge to catch the train about four in the morning. I remember queueing up. It was a long wait at London Bridge station. All hop pickers' special trains.

The station was packed with families and all the belongings

they had collected throughout the year for their stay 'down
hopping'. The scene was chaotic. Morning light barely break-
ing, the noise of tired, over-excited children and the anxious
mothers responsible, as ever, for their multiple chores: safe
keeping of the luggage; preventing offspring from going too
close to the railway lines; arbitrating between squabbling
youngsters.

We went down once on the hoppers' train. Aw! What a
palaver! . . . and me brothers left me, as I thought. I was
about seven or eight, a little 'un. And do you know them fish
bags they used to have? Made of straw with like a skewer
through the top. Well anyway, my brothers picked up what
bags they gotta have. She [her mother] only come on the
hoppers' train 'cos the boys wanted to. You had to be up, and
up the bleeding railway station at two in the morning. And
there's me struggling along with this bag, and me saying [little
girl's voice], 'That's it, you pick up the lighter stuff. Leave me
the heaviest one.' And I'm scraping it along the floor. Well
the train never went, and there's this porter running up and
down the platform at London Bridge, and he's saying,
'Somebody's picked hold of a bag of fish. Who's pinched the
fish?' So, of course, I never said nothing. Instead, I'm saying
to me mum, 'They left me with this heavy bag.' So *she* said,
'Shut up moaning.' My brother lifts up the bag and puts it in
the carriage and me mum said, 'Here's a stink of fish in this
carriage.' So I said, 'Oooooh!' She looked down and said,
'That's not my bag.' I'd left her bag on the platform and I'd
got the bleeding fish. No wonder it was heavy! *Mrs AB*

In the days before mass ownership of cars, hoppers who
chose neither to walk nor to use public transport needed to use
their initiative. One solution was to 'club together' to hire a
lorry for the excursion. The trip was usually undertaken very
early in the morning or at night, because the vehicle would
probably belong to a local tradesperson, who used it during the
day for its official purpose. The owner might not even be aware

of the 'moonlighting' activities of the driver. (This again is part of a popular story in many families' repertoires of hopping stories.) For some owners the annual hiring of their truck was part of their normal trading.

We used to come in old X's lorry. Out of the turning round the corner. He was a greengrocer. Took a load of families from round here. *Mrs C*

. . . it would all be dumped into the back of the lorry . . . it was Y's. You know, the old furniture dealers. It was all right though, you know, they used to hire that to take us then come back and pick us up. We always went on the back of a lorry. The men up the front would have a few bottles, and us and the young 'uns would hang out the back of the lorry. Legs dangling over the tailboard. *Mrs A*

The lorry used to come round and stop outside your house. All down the road. Used to pick us all up . . . We went with Lil and Winnie. Winnie must have had eleven kids . . . Lil had her two and me mum had us lot. So we'd all go down. All of us on the lorry. *Mrs RR*

Going by lorry was obviously a lot of fun for many of the women, who have fond memories of 'larking about', the 'lovely weather', and the frequent stops made whenever the passengers were 'thirsty'. Some of the trips turned into mobile parties.

I'm not sure how the piano got there. It must've been someone's furniture van that we'd 'borrowed'. But what I do know is we had a right old jolly up on the way down there. What with the piano and all of us! *Mrs S*

Used to take the piano on the back of the lorry. Down hopping! Bloody great Alsatian dogs, canaries, all sorts! A right turn out! *Mrs T*

However the Londoners managed it, on foot, by train, on the back of a lorry, in a cart, or by Green Line bus, they eventually arrived in the Garden of England. Their next job was to settle in and get 'their' huts ready for the stay down hopping.

3
Arriving and Settling In

'It was home from home.'

The standard of accommodation provided for the 'foreigners' (the name given to the Londoners by the 'home dwellers' – the locals who picked) was primitive and overcrowded. This, however, is when it is compared with what is considered acceptable by most people in Britain today. The conditions that working class families experienced in their daily lives in east London, particularly during the post-war years, were probably not a lot better than those 'down hopping'. It is important to remember the context of that period in the lives of the women when they reminisce about how they lived and worked in the often squalid conditions of the hop farms. The women were, usually, relatively poor; many lived close to the docks and would have experienced some form of war damage to their own, their families' or their neighbours' homes; the bulk of their domestic labour would have been completed, as it is today, within individual households, in monotonous isolation. These factors obviously had an effect on how they reacted to their temporary homes in the Kent countryside.

Realising, for instance, that most of the women's homes would have lacked a bathroom is a useful pointer to understanding how families coped with the lack of facilities in Kent. At the time when all of the women were still picking, even basic indoor plumbing was a luxury only to be dreamt of, or seen at the pictures in the latest Hollywood film. Mrs T was the only woman I spoke to who had a bathroom by the beginning of the war. Her family had been moved to a flat, on a new 'model' housing estate, which had bathrooms as standard fittings. She recalled inviting friends round to have a bath, mainly to show them the novelty of having hot running water on tap. Similarly, Mrs R, a 'scholarship girl', had been so impressed by the bathroom of one of her new, middle class school friends, that she still remembers the awe with which she and another working class girl discussed the 'fur toilet'. Mrs R now laughs at how they were so easily amazed by a fluffy, candlewick bathroom mat, and how the room had seemed so exotic, just because it had a plumbed-in bath and an indoor lavatory. She also laughed when admitting that she might miss some things, but definitely not the night-time trips to the bottom of the garden, nor the ferrying of buckets of hot water from the copper boiler to the tin bath. Her experiences were like those of the majority of poorer London women; most domestic labour was unaided by technology, although this was to change rapidly in the post-war years.

They might have owned few valuable material possessions, but the women all talked about the pride they took in preparing their huts and settling in. Having the hut look as nice as possible was important if your temporary neighbours were to see you as a respectable family. 'Proper' women would get on with the job of organising their huts and would not leave their hopping boxes unpacked for too long, but first they had to greet all their old friends.

You'd get to the farm, and you'd see them all. One'd come up to the other and say 'Hello so-and-so!' And you hadn't seen them for a year. Since last year! We was always brought up as kids to call 'em aunts, and that. *Mrs AB*

You'd meet all your old friends . . . all your old friends that you'd left last hopping, wouldn't you? *Mrs D*

Same old faces! *Mrs S*

The huts were often given to the same family each year. This made it easier for the regulars, who could leave large items on the farm; it also gave them more opportunities to personalise the huts with their own decorations.

Every year we'd do something a bit different to the hut. New bit of wallpaper. Few more cups on the old dresser. Shelves up. Lace curtains changed. *Mrs M*

When I visited Mrs D in her London house, she had some beautiful china displayed on dressers. She took the dishes and plates on her journeys to and from Kent every year – it was too precious for her to leave in London or in the hut.

You used to get your hut. We had the same one every year. You'd have your own hut if you was a regular. But oh! they was like sheds! Stables are better. Take the odd rolls of wallpaper and stick them up. Or a bit of, well, it used to be distemper in them days. You'd fill a couple of bed ticks with straw and sew 'em up. Put your faggots down first, then lay more straw on the ledge like. Yeh, you'd use the tea chests, that you took your gear in, for a table. Pots and pans and me bit of china. Take that home and bring it down when we went. A few lace curtains. Used to take a bit of lace curtain to put round the door and round me bed. Make it like a four poster. Old bit of mat down. The boys used to get me that. They used to go out calling [rag and bone collecting], didn't they?

The huts needed a lot of work to transform them into family homes. They were very basic.

It was just galvanised. Bit over the roof and a wooden door. Bit cut out of the top of the door – so big [about 18 inches] – and that was it! Your light and ventilation. But I had a beautiful photo of my mother standing up on the bed looking out of the hop hut window. Like this. [Mimes her mother peering through the space cut out of the top of the door. Laughter.] And then some of them had proper windows. You could have your lace curtains round them lovely big windows . . . My sister-in-law's family was in the huts behind. The wooden ones. And they was Catholic see, her people. And you can hear everything in them huts. No privacy! See, and my old mum said, 'Gor blimey!', she said; 'What's that light?' She looked out the door and saw their huts. I looked out and they was all alight. Course, my sister-in-law's saying, 'Say your Marys, say your Marys.' And my mum didn't swear, but she shouted out, '*Sod* your Marys. Get down there and help get them kids out!' I'll never forget it. Aw my Gawd! (laughter) '*Sod* your Marys!' *Mrs AB*

As can be seen from Mrs AB's point about the windows, even within the low standard of hoppers' accommodation, there were variations from farm to farm.

Mrs T: They had two huts. Separated up between all their kids. Inside! Didn't have a lot of space.

Mrs RR: Ours were proper huts, where we went. Made out of wood. Proper huts.

Mrs T: [Mock posh] *Ours* were brick.

But whatever they were like, the huts were to be the family home for the picking season. Getting organised for country life was important for everyone's comfort.

Panic! The kids'd be pushed to one side to take all the small bits, the rest was taken in by their elders. First we used to lay out the straw like, as you used to go into the huts. You had a long bit along here, then you used to lay the straw out there. [Miming the waist-high shelf at the far end of the hut on which the bed, for all the family, would be made up.] Me nan had a mattress, a proper one, but we had these bolsters, for pillows, that we had to fill with the straw . . . I'd put all the kitchen stuff away . . . then we had the job of doing the jam jars. Tying string around, sticking half jam and water in it, and sticking them on nails outside the huts . . . keep the wasps and flies away. There's me nan and grandad on the mattress, then me and me aunt. But she was the same age and size as me. We was at the bottom. Me two uncles, both kids, were on the floor with stuffed ticks. And I think all the rest of the kids was mingled in with the rest of me family and other families in the other huts. But I know our hut was normally full of bodies. You know, sleeping here, there and every-where . . . our huts were wood, not corrugated iron, because I remember when we put the jam jars up we could knock a nail in. Just the base of the bit where me nan slept was concrete. Like the shelf affair . . . You'd go straight in and come straight out! No windows. Cor, it was ever so dark, wasn't it? The only light we had was the candles. In little curly things, like Rip Van Winkle. Not even Tilly lamps in our hut. *Mrs AA*

With the number of children running around, the wooden huts and the straw-stuffed beds, candles must have been a constant fire threat. Mrs C said that her hut had more technolo-gically advanced facilities.

G: What lighting did you have?

Mrs C: Used to have an oil lamp. But then I got a proper Tilly lamp. And that was a fortune. One year's hopping money then. Five pounds.

G: Like having the electric laid on!

Mrs C: I bought it in the co-op and they posted it down here to me. That was marvellous having a Tilly lamp. It *was* like having electric light.

The huts were a source of pride and, at times, a basis for competition between the women. They could demonstrate that they were 'respectable'; that they were women who cared about their surroundings. Some of the women went to great lengths in the very limited circumstances to make the huts as pleasant and comfortable as possible.

We had lino, carpet, the lot. China. Take your wellingtons off before you went in the hut. I've got this posh brother. Well, fancies he is. Lord Rothschild! Lace curtains, valance round the edge of the bed. Like a little manger. We had two hop huts. Always the same huts for her and the kids. Dad used to come at the weekends. She used to keep them lovely. Wallpaper and everything. They were good huts, wooden *and* with windows. Some places used to have them galvanised tin huts. No ventilation or nothing. That's right. Ours were off the floor. Them tin ones went straight on to the floor. Some of the kids used to get fevers. That farm I told you about had them huts right till they stopped picking. Along by the pub there. They was just galvanised tin, straight on to the floor. We used to have our huts off the ground. A proper shelf at one end for the bed. We slept top-to-toe. Mum and the youngest kids in one hut, the older boys in the other. She always had two huts, my mum . . . Then we'd get the faggots to light the fire, and hang the pots on. Boil up and we was all settled in! *Mrs AB*

I had curtains everywhere. A proper calor gas stove. Wallpaper. We pasted ours up properly too, none of them drawing pins. We hardboarded the walls inside and wallpapered it fresh every year. And painted the ceiling. We did that. It was home from home! Only thing was, you had more fresh air. More than here, more *out*! *Mrs C*

The huts were arranged carefully to be just what Mrs C described as 'home from home', for that was what they had to be for the picking season. The sanitation arrangements, how-

ever, had to be accepted as part of the country way of life.
Lavatories are a prominent part of all the recollections including mine. Even those women who have only vague memories
from early childhood all remembered the lavatories.

Don't talk to me about the loos! They were really horrible. No
bucket or nothing. Just a hole dug, with one of the chestnut
poles across. [The poles used for supporting the growing
hops.] And you'd have to hold on to that pole. *Mrs AB*

This balancing act was a fairly common arrangement. Sometimes it, and our modesty, was sheltered by some sort of fencing
or hut-like construction.

Like a workman's shed with a hole in and a pole propped
across. And they was a little way away from the huts too. You
used to have to leave in time to get there. [Laughing] And
when you think! I suppose everybody bloody used it . . . I
can remember having the runs! [Laughter] Trying to get to it,
and then balancing on that pole, and all that bleeding mud.
Awww. I was only young, and when you start wanting a bit of
privacy. *Mrs RR*

Other farms had slightly more refined, if not more hygienic,
sanitary arrangements.

Well we had a little hut, all on its own with a drum in it. And
we used to go on that. Someone would come and empty it
every now and then. Go and empty it somewhere across the
fields . . . I can remember, with my little fishing net – not
going down the stream where we took the Lifebuoy [to wash]
– but there was this lake. It was filled with these little green
leaves, whatever they're called, and there were all these big
black things floating on it. I thought they was prunes, and I
picked up a couple. And I eat them! And I remember I had
the old diarrhoea! They were like a black pod and for some
reason I thought they was prunes. But they gave me the

bellyache and the poohs! And we only had that drum for a lav! *Mrs AA*

The local authorities were concerned officially about the conditions in which the pickers worked and were housed – they were obliged to be so. The Ministry of Health had issued model by-laws related to the environment in which the hoppers lived during the picking season. Health visitors called at the farms to check on the situation, but they were not always welcomed. Sometimes the women would have adapted the huts for added comfort at the expense of meeting the by-law requirements. Mrs C recalled a visit made by officers of Kent County Council:

They came round to inspect all the huts, and one year, you know all the ruts in the corrugated iron roof? Because it was cold, they'd all stuffed 'em up. And he stood there and pulled every bit out. Because there wouldn't have been no ventilation. That was before they put any windows in. See now you look at my hut . . . where the bottom bit of board was, I always had that open. That was your air . . . You'd block it up when it was cold, but when it was hot it was worse than an oven, see, really.

The huts certainly became hot and stuffy if the day was sunny, but often the mornings were quite cold. This would have a definite effect on the morning ablutions, especially if your farmer expected you to wash in the stream at the bottom of the field.

When we got up of a morning – the kids, like – I don't think we ever washed. Not us older ones. We was *meant* to. Too early and too cold. I can remember having a wash down of a night, but not in the mornings. *Mrs T*

We'd get up between half five and six. 'Cos it was early, me and the other kids never wanted to get up. Brrr [shivering] we'd go down to that stream, bar of Lifebuoy. Carbolic

Lifebuoy! We were supposed to wash but we never did. Come back and put on whatever we were wearing. And wellies. All that mud. *Mrs A*

The summers of our memories might be golden but the mud wasn't. Mud was as much a part of daily life on the hop farms as the children avoiding their morning wash.

It was all right if it was dry. When it rained it was terrible! Mud everywhere. Awful. *Mrs RL*

But even with the mud, the unsanitary lavatories, cold mornings and carbolic soap, the women were glad to be 'down hopping' and settled into their own huts. Mrs C spoke about a year when the women did not even get their huts to themselves, but still they were glad to be there, to be back:

The farmer had to wait for the ground to settle before he could get some of the huts finished off. Before the floors could be done. They were running alive with rats. Nothing you could do about it. And everyone was so keen to be there that they shared the huts there was. So eager to come hopping that you never thought about anything like that till you come.

It didn't seem to matter that it was a bit cold when the women had to get up for work in the hop gardens, for most of them central heating was as distant a luxury as fitted kitchens and bathrooms.

Mrs RR: It was autumn, but I can remember we used to have some beautiful weather at times. But it was nippy of a morning, and the nights were drawing in. But I still say now, 'It's like hopping morning.' When it's bright and fresh. Lovely mornings. Sometimes a low mist. Lovely.

Mrs T: Birds all singing.

Mrs RR: Yeh, well we'd have never seen countryside unless you went down there.

Mrs T: It was like a foreign land wasn't it?

Mrs AB knew why women continued to go hopping. Even though it was hard, dirty, low paid, casual employment, with difficult, unpleasant conditions in which to live, Mrs AB knew why they went:

Well, you didn't take no notice of all that because you were happy!

And so the families arrived after their journeys; organised what was to be called 'home' for the next six weeks or so; boiled some water for a cup of tea to share with old friends; and generally settled into their huts which had been transformed by odd rolls of wallpaper and a coat of distemper. But the women did not have long to relax in their temporary country residences.

Oh! Only today. Picking tomorrow! *Mrs C*

4
The Day's Work

They say that hopping's lousy
I don't believe it's true
We only go down hopping to earn a bob or two
With a tee aye oh, a tee aye oh, a tee aye ee aye oh!

(Traditional hopping song)

Apart from some minor innovations, such as training the bines up strings rather than poles, there have been few changes in the techniques by which hops are grown. In many ways the women I spoke to would have felt 'at home' working alongside the hoppers of the nineteenth century. The Victorian workers would certainly be familiar with the cycle of planting and growing that still takes place today – the patterns that are repeated every season, year in, year out. The time to gather the hops still depends on the weather and the varieties favoured by the farmer, but with the introduction of machinery, harvesting has changed dramatically. The fields are no longer filled with busy hoppers and their children.

The actual duration of the hand-picking season always varied, but the daily routine did not. Each morning the workers were called, whistled, or 'blown on' to the fields by the bailiff or farm manager. The blowing on was done with a traditional horn-type instrument. On the first day, the rules would usually then be read out to the assembled pickers and pole pullers (or binmen). The detailed rules would also appear on the back of the pickers' accounts books, but it was not assumed that all pickers could read.

The most usual method of picking in Kent was for family

groups to strip the hop cones off the bines and into the hop bins. The hop bins were large sacking bags supported by poles, which rested on end trestles. The pole pullers used long thin poles topped with a sharp blade to cut free the bines and pull them down for the pickers to 'clean' into the bins. In some areas, such as parts of east Kent, hops were picked directly into the bushel measuring baskets.

The pole puller was responsible for ensuring that all the bins in his set (a set was a group of bins, varying in number) were kept supplied with bines to strip. Practically without exception, this task was performed by men, sometimes by Londoners working with their own families.

It might be an older son who got this job, or less often, the picker's husband would take the work if employment couldn't be found 'back home' in London. Dockers, for instance, in the days before the Dock Labour Scheme was introduced, were at the mercy of the notoriously unreliable and dehumanising casual system, and would often be glad of being employed as pole pullers if work was slack. (Tragically, for many workers, the Dock Labour Scheme was scrapped in 1989.) During the war years however, women, including Land Army 'girls', did pole pulling when there was a shortage of male labour. Many examples of industries 'making do' with female labour during war time have been well documented elsewhere.

Unlike the hop pickers, who worked on piece rates, pole pullers received an agreed daily fee for the duration of their temporary employment. This regular wage made pole pulling an attractive prospect, and there would be bad feelings if a local man who wanted the job was not given priority over a 'foreign' applicant.

Feelings were not all that could be hurt. The bines were covered in harsh prickles which became particularly fierce when the dew had dried from them. At the beginning of the picking season, hands that had become unused to the work during the year since the last harvest would be scratched until they bled. Some women chose to wear gloves, but these slowed down the rate at which they could pick, so their earnings would be less.

At regular intervals during the day the measurers, or tally men, would go around measuring and recording how many hops had been picked into each bin. The measurers were always regular farm employees and almost invariably male. Their responsibility was to the farmer. They checked the number of bushels by filling the measure, a bushel basket, from the bin. Each measure of hops was then emptied into the poke, a ten bushel sack, ready to be taken to the oast houses for drying. The number of bushels picked into each bin were tallied, or entered into the hoppers' accounts books. These books would have been unfamiliar to Victorian hoppers who would have expected their measurers to hand them a token, or mark a tally stick. Whatever the method used by the measurers, it was against this record of their labour that the pickers would claim their wages at the end of the harvest. If they needed to, and were fortunate enough to have an understanding employer, the hop pickers could get a 'sub', which would be deducted from their total. This, of course, depended on the farmer and his relationship with the hoppers.

The working day lasted from about seven in the morning until about five in the evening, when the cry, 'Pull no more bines' was called through the fading light of the hop fields.

Mrs D described a day typical of those experienced by hoppers over many years of harvesting; a day that would be recognised by most people who have been hopping:

You used to get up in the morning. I'd have the water boiled, the tea made and a big plate of toast for all the kids. Then I'd do the basket. Pack our bit of food in it. Fill the kettle up with water and take it up the field for our breakfast time. Used to cut our breakfast up on the field. I had pictures of me mum doing it. Getting the breakfast on the fields, just like I did it for my kids. Big arm basket full of grub. And er, nine o'clock, we'd boil the kettle. We'd work from seven to nine. He'd blow you on, work till nine and have a cup of tea and something to eat. He used to have a horn. Used to blow it and you'd start. At seven. And then he'd come round, the measurer, measure the hops after breakfast. Then you'd work till dinner time. Half past twelve. They used to measure them by the bushel. We used to do bin picking. I remember when they was three bushels a shilling. It used to be hard then. But then working at it all your life, you're good ain't you? We always had four bins. Half past twelve to one you'd stop again. Then you'd work till five. He used to call you off at five. Yeh, measure your hops about half past four so you could pick a start for the morning.

The hop cones were easier to strip from the bines when they were still wet from the dew. As the day wore on, and if it was good weather, the dry prickles on the bines would feel harsher on the women's skin. The variety of hops also mattered.

Seven o'clock in the morning, all dressed up with the woolly hats and what have you, because it was cold of a morning. But by dinner time it used to be lovely. But I like picking hops first thing in the morning. They were wet and oh they were lovely to pick, wasn't they? . . . You just used to go like that with your finger to pull the leaves off. Shooosh! Like that. Into the bin. Course, being wet in the morning, lovely. But when they got dry. Prickles! And your hands got all brown. But it'd give you appetite. Make you sleep, and all. *Mrs M*

Mrs D: It was lovely picking when they was wet. They come off easy. I used to stand by the bin all day. Pick hops. I loved it.

G: It must have hurt your fingers.

Mrs D: Oh yeh. But your old hands, you used to get hardened.

G: Did you ever wear gloves?

Mrs D: *No*! Couldn't pick with gloves! In the war they grew some medical hops. They called them. We used to pick them. They used to tear your hands to pieces.

G: I've never heard of them.

Mrs D: Medical hops they was. They grew them in that one place, and we used to – we went over there and picked for 'em. Yeh. Just our family did it there. But as you used to pull the hops though. Aw! they used to cut your hands . . . they was medical hops. They was kept separate. We used to keep 'em all separate as they was picked. It was like a small piece of the farm, and he just had like us pick 'em. The bines was so rough. But they were great *big* hops though. Beautiful hops.

Mrs AB: It wasn't hard work, it was tiring. And the bines was really rough. You used to get scratched . . . when they tried growing them American hops though! Old Tom used to go round with plasters. They used to really cut you to bits.

G: Were they like the medical hops someone told me about?

Mrs AB: Yeh. Well, I don't know. But they used to cut your fingers to bits . . . they was special. Medical hops. Great big fat hops with spiky thorns.

I never did manage to find out what medical hops were. I've got a romantic notion that there are some things that are more interesting when they remain a bit mysterious. (It would be a real disappointment if 'medical hops' turned out to be a cockney mishearing of a countryman saying 'American hops'.)

Even seemingly unattractive aspects of hopping, like the wear and tear on their hands, were recalled fondly by some of the women, but the pleasure they all remembered was the happy, companionable way of working.

Sit on the bin. Talk. Pick. Talk. Have a cigarette, have a laugh. Have a good laugh while you carried on picking. We'd have a laugh! *Mrs C*

Mrs RR: It was a right lark, but what I didn't like was when you pulled the bine down all the bleeding spiders, and the dew, all over you. All up your sleeves. Yuch! Used to come

all over you, didn't it? And about six of us all picking around
the bin. All together, having a lark. Used to go everywhere.
[Laughing] And if you ate anything the first day, it was all
bitter, wasn't it? Me mum used to have a go. Used to say that
I was old enough to pick. And it you wanted a couple of bob,
you've got to do it. A lot of the time she used to sit us in the
bin with all the bleeding hops!

G: That's my earliest memory I've got of hopping, the smell
of the hops all around you while you're sitting in the bin. I
can still smell that smell now. [Pause] I can't remember the
taste on the food though.

Mrs RR: . . . Remember them pop bottles that used to have
the er, the stopper on like a wire cage thing? Cork used to be
pushed in. Like a china stopper.

Mrs C: And how about eating sandwiches with your hoppy
hands?

Mrs ML: Lovely. Make 'em taste better. Make the cheese
and onion taste all the better!

Mrs S: At first I couldn't. When we'd just got started, I used
to wrap a bit of newspaper round it, then eat it. *Then* I could
eat it.

By the time me nan was ready, with her headscarf, her apron
and her half knee socks, we'd follow her down. All of us kids
. . . We used to have our bit of breakfast when we got down
there . . . Me nan, me aunties . . . all picking together . . . I
did love that. And I *love* the smell of hops! . . . I can smell
the hops, and I can see it all . . . I'd go off with the other kids
on the back of the tractor. To me it was just a big adventure.
Going down on the back of the tractor with the big sacks.
Down to where they dried them. Then coming back on the
empty tractor. Me poor old nan would've started another bin.
Mrs AA

The women's experiences became more varied when we spoke about the importance that families placed on how much work was actually done during the day – how many hops were actually picked. They also disagreed about how much the children were expected to contribute to the family tally. Even with a large family, Mrs AB's mother would only ever have two bins, compared with Mrs D's four.

Fourteen kids she'd make breakfast for! [All members of her extended family.] And she used to stand there as we had our breakfast and she used to say, 'Go on, get down there on them bins.' We had two bins . . . Down we used to go. But Mum never made us pick. But *her*. [A neighbour] She'd have a bit of bine on the bin, and if they dared look up the fields she used to [mimes hitting the children] and, 'Pick them hops!' She did. They wasn't allowed to move from that bin. Sometimes one of my mum's bins'd be empty all day. I was the same with my kids. Like my mum. I never made 'em pick. I used to say, 'Pick me one box full, then you can go and play.' They used to about half fill it. A little box. And that was it. They'd tip it in the bin before I could look. Or so they thought . . . No, I never made them pick. *Mrs AB*

Some of the kids were made to pick but we were spoilt. Some'd get a clip round the ear if they didn't pick. Not us. But we did our fair share. Or what *we* thought was our fair share. Nan used to work hard for her money, but I could never say that I grafted. Not like she worked . . . There were a lot of kids, believe it or not, who didn't pick a thing. Never helped at all. We thought we was hard done by at the time 'cos we had to pick a couple of hops. Now, when I think how hard my nan had to work. *Mrs AA*

Mrs S was one of the women who remembered being forced to work:

I had to pick a bucket for my mum. All of us kids did. She made us. And you wouldn't dare move until you had.

The children's ages obviously affected how much the adults expected of them. Until the school leaving age was raised to 15, 13- and 14-year-olds would probably already be in some sort of paid employment at home; if they went hopping they would be expected to work (even if they didn't always do so). It was usually the girls who continued going to Kent with their mothers even after they had started at a regular job; the boys would stay at home with the other adult males of the family, going to Kent just for weekend visits. Some full-time employers would sack boys when they reached 16, as they would then merit a higher 'man's' wage. If that happened the boy might accompany his mother and younger brothers and sisters, even perhaps getting a pole puller's job.

The girls of my age. Teenagers then! We'd all go down and pick. *Mrs T*

See, if we picked a few, me mum would give us a few coppers. But we still used to get fed up. We'd want the money, but we'd slope off. *Mrs RR*

The smaller children were easier to control. It was not unusual to see under fives sitting in the bins pulling single hops, one by one, from the bines. My earliest memory of hopping is just that: sitting deep in the hessian bin, surrounded by dew-wet bines, stripping hop cones from the prickly stalks; getting even wetter as the water fell on my head and shoulders as the pole puller dragged the next lot down around me. I can recall, with the genuine pleasure of feeling secure and happy, the bitter smell of hops any time that I think of that scene. More adventurous or slightly older children would be attached to the wooden bin supports with a length of rope, tethered like little ponies, to stop them wandering off into the unknown dangers of the Kent countryside. Those same children, like me, probably had a far more dangerous playground in London. At that age, a bombsite, the Regent's Canal, a major road and the railway line formed the four boundaries of my known world. Yet my mum and the other women were more concerned about the pastoral mysteries threatening their offspring.

The reins were always long enough to allow the children to move around and to help the family by collecting any loose hops that had fallen to the ground.

They'd send the little kids up and down the row, picking up the bits here and there. *Mrs D*

Sometimes we'd throw them into an upturned umbrella! *Mrs S*

These loose hops were more keenly gathered if the measurer was on his way to your bin. They could make the difference between getting the tally – or not – for another bushel. One of the most popular hopping songs was rendered in a variety of moods, depending on the tally.

Our lovely hops, our lovely hops
When the measurer he comes round
Pick 'em up, pick 'em up off the ground
When he starts to measure he don't know when to stop
Aye aye get in the bin and take the blooming lot!

That was Mrs C's version of the song and the one which had the most polite words. Other versions expressed just how much power the measurer had over the pickers, and how strongly they felt about the fairness, or not, of the authority he wielded. If he wanted to, the measurer could pack the hops down firmly into the basket, meaning that the pickers had to pick far more hops to get a bushel tallied and recorded on their card.

Sometimes the measurer'd stick 'em in a bit heavy, and the old dears would say, 'Why don't you stick 'em in with your feet?' . . . Some of the hoppers would chuck in all sorts of bits to fill up the basket. But some of the measurers weren't fair. Some of the pokes you'd see were like a football. Some of the others, if they were from the home dwellers' bins, was flat. *Mrs AB*

The measurer was usually seen by the Londoners as favouring the locals, the resentment focusing on him as a regular farm employee who knew the home dwellers personally. Job allocation was seen as being based on whether a person was local or not. It was also recognised that jobs were gender specific. Mrs M's husband worked as a pole puller while he was staying with his aunt.

Mr M: 'Come on,' she said, 'there's a pole pulling job.' So I had a pole pulling job while I was staying with her. It was my holiday. That was always a man's job. Always. Tradition I suppose.

G: And it paid more?

Mr M: Yeh. That was seen as a man's wages.

G: Did the pole pullers ever do measuring?

Mr M: No! That was a separate job. They wouldn't allow a pole puller to do that. Because he'd have his own family there, and then if you did measure there, naturally you'd only put in half. They was fly to all that! You *never* got Londoners or that measuring. That was always the regular workers on the farm to do the measuring. But you could earn good money pole pulling. I did, when I did the fortnight's pole pulling that I got. I earned good money.

According to Mrs AB, the farmers were probably wise not to use the pole pullers as measurers:

See, they used to go down hopping and take these pole pulling jobs if they was on the run. Down from London or somewhere. And they never thought they'd be found out . . . He was on the run [a pole puller]. *You* know. The place was swarming with police . . . But they never did catch him! [Laughter]

As might be expected, it was only in exceptional circumstances that the traditional, and usually unquestioned, gender division was defied.

The men didn't used to pick . . . some of the older boys maybe did . . . but the men used to do the pulling of the poles. You know, at the top to get the bines down? I remember going during the war. There wasn't no men then. Women did the pole pulling and that then. *Mrs D*

Its always been the women who did the picking. The only time we had men picking was in the thirties. When they was all on the unemployed. When the Strike and that was on. Lot of young chaps come down and had a bin then. *Farmer D*

So, apart from these odd times, picking was seen as, and accepted as, women's and children's work; pole pulling as men's. The wages were higher for the men, but still lower than could be earned in London, relegating the women's earnings from picking to an even lowlier category.

The older men – if they went – were on the poles. But the young ones, the kids, used to pick. The pole pulling was more money 'cos it was men's work. When they weren't drinking. *Mrs AA*

The men was pole pullers. J was our pole puller for years and years. He come from Bow . . . He was there for years. But remember, if the men had work they stayed in London, 'cos you couldn't earn enough here. *Mrs C*

Some London men come down as pole pullers. Men *never* picked. *No!* Pole pullers. They'd never pick. No. That was women's jobs. They could have used local men, but some London men still come to do the pole pulling. *Mrs AB*

The London men weren't always able to get employment on

the farms even if they wanted it. This again could lead to resentment about farmers favouring local people at the expense of Londoners.

The locals used to kick up a right old fuss if the pole pulling was given to Londoners. That was regular wages. You've got to understand that. *Mrs J*

If Dad was on leave he used to pick, because it was really hard to get on the pole pulling. It was the money see? No, the pole pulling was really hard to get on . . . See, before the war, when work was harder, he might go down. Get a bit of pole pulling if he could. That was decent money. Earn a few bob. But after the war Dad always worked. It wasn't worth it for him to go down and pick then. The men stayed at their work if they could, see. *Mrs RR*

The potential for women to earn a decent wage was further reduced by the introduction of new strains of hop plant:

Well it had been 10 to 12 pence a bushel. I don't remember exactly, but it wasn't much money . . . and then these new hops, they're so small. You had to pick so many to get a bushel. I mean, you're picking, picking, picking. *Mrs C*

With all the barriers to earning even a miserly amount, the women still considered it worthwhile to leave whatever paid employment they had in London, or to 'fiddle' extra time off from their jobs.

I'd go on holiday for two weeks. Then go sick! Go sick for four weeks, or how long hopping lasted . . . They knew I went hop picking. Sometimes I'd ask for just a week, I'd go back down to London for the day, *then* I'd be sick. And come back down hopping! *Mrs ML*

If women gave up their regular employment in London it was

not always easy to get another job. Not all employers chose to turn the blind eye favoured by Mrs ML's employer. Some women had to find ways of dealing with the prejudice against taking on 'hopping girls'. Mrs D used her imagination and acting ability to get a job for the winter from which she could eventually go sick:

I remember I came home once and went for a job down at K's factory. 'Yeh,' he said, 'Yeh, I'll start you in the morning. You can start in the boiler house.' But then he looked at my hands. They'd do that. And he said, 'You've been hopping!' You could always tell if you'd been hopping, you couldn't get that horrible, browny-black stain off from the resin. I said, 'Yeh, that's right.' 'Well,' he said, 'You won't leave us for hopping?' I said, 'No! I'll stop here for ever. If I get the job.' I thought – yeh, that's right, once I've got the job, I'm off down hopping.

Workers' resistance of a different kind was feared by the farmers. The harvest could be disrupted if the hoppers decided to act collectively. A farmer told me about the following difficulties experienced by his neighbours:

We never had hoppers' strikes here, but I know they had at Manwaring's and Kennard's. Oh Kennard's used to strike every year. Wouldn't be down here five minutes and they'd be on strike. 'Cos you want to remember there'd be a thousand huts there, Kennard's used to have. Just over that bridge there, a thousand huts. The strike'd be over the tally, you know. Oh yeh, every year: 'Kennard's are on strike!' Only two days on. No that was nothing unusual, not there!

Nobody I spoke to was involved in strikes, probably because they were all employed on relatively small farms where the relationships between farmers and pickers was more personal. But there are documented strikes which took place from the nineteenth century onwards. Local newspapers would frequently carry stories about these actions which were typically the result of complaints about the standards of accommodation, pay and conditions. Later strikes resulted from the hoppers' understandable mistrust of the machinery which was being introduced by their employers.

When all was going smoothly, however, and the women had picked for a full day's wages, work would stop in the hop garden at about five o'clock. No more bines were to be pulled. The final measuring of the day had been completed and the last pokes were being taken to the oast houses on the back of a cart, horses or tractor pulling it across the rutted earth. The women would walk back through the hop gardens to their huts on the grassy 'common', carrying their youngest children, their empty baskets and kettles. The older children might help their mothers, or run ahead, chasing their friends, loving the freedom of the fields. But it wasn't yet time for the women to relax – they had more work to do. Twilight would be approaching; fires and lamps had to be lit before it got too dark; food and laundry had to be organised. Chores never stopped, not even down hopping.

5
The Evenings

'We made our own entertainment.'

Memories about the routine domestic chores carried out by women down hopping make the work seem as unchanging as hopping itself once seemed to be. The ages of the women who spoke to me (see Part 2 for brief biographical details) show that their own memories of hop picking begin close to 1920, but the dates of the stories are not so easily placed. The stories they tell are not only about their own experiences, they also recall tales told by their mothers and grandmothers. This adds to the timeless quality of 'going down hopping'. Related to this sense of timelessness, it is interesting how many of the women's own stories were from their childhood – memories about being daughters. Even though the women had gone hop picking as adults, and had taken their own children to Kent, their most vivid recollections were of when they were girls. This was particularly noticeable when they spoke about the domestic work carried out by the women, their mothers and grand-mothers, in the evenings.

> *Mrs D*: Time you got home and had a wash. You'd get all the wood. [The bundles of twigs known as faggots.] On'd go all the pots, and Mum'd cook us a nice hot tea. The girls'd wash up. We had a nice big fire. The beds'd be made. It used to get

really dark by about eight didn't it? Then we'd have a big fire outside, and sit talking till it was time to go to bed.

G: That was when you were with your mum. How about when you were the mum?

Mrs D: Just the same. Carry on just the same. Yeh. Same jobs, just the same.

The women managed to produce a 'nice hot tea' for their children with very basic equipment, just the hopping pot – a cast iron cauldron – suspended over an open fire. Some farms did provide cookhouses but these were usually so smoke-filled that the women preferred to cook in the open air outside their huts. There was also a sense of pride that the women used their own private utensils and facilities.

Whatever you could do in the hopping pot, you had that. Anything you could do in the old iron boiler, wasn't it? Bit of bacon, nice meat pudding used to do. Nice big pot of stew. Or we'd have chops, something like that, with taters and greens. All that. All on the outside fire. Always on our own fire, 'cos we used to have, you know, our own stuff. And we had our own kettle prop . . . stick it in the ground and the kettle used to hook over the fire. It was like cleaner to use your own gear. You'd know where it'd been and that! *Mrs D*

We'd have whatever was being cooked. I remember we used to have a lot of stews and that – anything that could go in the pot. Anything that Nan had. But it always come out nice, everything she did for us. *Mrs A*

We had a great big pot. Had it for bleeding donkey's years. We always cooked round the fire. It used to be lousy in the cookhouse. All smoky. We used to like to sit round the fire and do ours. Didn't like that dirty cookhouse. *Mrs RR*

Yeh, in the hopping pot it'd all go. Stick it all in and stew it all up. Lovely dinners you'd have out of it. All out of the one pot and all. *Mrs S*

The women had to use their ingredients in unconventional ways, to suit the peculiar restrictions presented by cooking in a single pot over an open, faggot-fuelled fire.

Of a night. Corned beef stew. Lovely! Sausage stew. Bit of boiled bacon. Nothing elaborate. Whatever would go in the hopping pot. *Mrs T*

You'd even do a roast in the pot. Potatoes in the bottom, a pot roast. And I used to make a Yorkshire pudding in a frying pan, and put currants in it . . . and I'm not being funny but I like Yorkshire pudding fried. Then I could do bubble in the morning, with a bit of bacon. *Mrs C*

Tea drinking was a serious business. Plenty of hot tea was available at all times. This was achieved by keeping a constantly refilled billy can of the brew boiling over the fire, both outside the hut in the evenings and close by the bins during the day. This last practice was frowned on by the farmers, due to the risk of sparks spreading the fire to the bines, but still the brewing-up continued. Tea drinking formed a regular punctuation to the working days and evenings round the fire.

And, of course, the billy would be boiling with the milk and sugar already in it. Yuch! The big billy full of tea and tin mugs. You'd scoop the tea out of it. Oooooh! horrible. The tea was really vile like that. *Mrs A*

It was vile that tea. All stewed. And all sweet. Corrr, horrible! *Mrs S*

Most of us shared Mrs A's opinion of the tea made and served in this way. Nobody liked it but the practice continued. None of us could think why, except to say that that was the way our mum had done it – 'boiling it up over the faggot fire'. The women also did their washing that way, using the fire and a big pot as their outdoor laundry.

Mrs C: What did I do with the napkins and knickers?

Mrs ML: Stick 'em in the big pot and boil 'em.

Mrs C: And peg 'em up in the cookhouse overnight so as they, you know . . . mind you, the smoke. You'd have to wash some of it again . . . Washing? We boiled up on the fire, all the hot water was there that we needed. You'd fill up and boil up. You done your washing.

Having clean clothes, especially white things, was seen as a sign of respectability – an important issue for grandmothers, mothers *and* daughters. The women all spoke with pride about the standard of cleanliness they managed to achieve with such basic equipment.

I used to go hopping with my babies with white napkins. I'd get an old tin bath, light the fire, with like a brick each end. Put on the bath and my napkins used to be like snow. Boil 'em up. Used to be beautiful. Yeh. Used to be lovely. They'd be all blowing. I used to hang 'em out on the trees. *Mrs D*

Nan always took her washboard. She always packed that, that went on the lorry. And a big tub. Used to fill it with cold water and hot water'd be poured on from the fire. She used to use Lux soap flakes. Hang it on lines from one hut to another. And that washing was *always* clean. And the ironing, one of them old spit-on-it, you know. Stick it on the fire to heat up. When my nan left that hut it was spotless. It was like when we went in. It was spotless. We had the same hut every year. Ours was the end one. The washing line we put up went right from our corner right the way to the next block. They used to get the hand washing ever so clean. The whitest thing I've ever had was my socks. Pure white. *Mrs A*

Once the chores had been finished the women could relax for a while. They could sit around the fires outside the huts, talking, singing and laughing. The youngest children safely tucked up asleep in the huts behind them, the older children using the farm as their playground.

And all the singsongs round the fire, the mums and that. I always remember them evenings, and we'd, the kids – I don't know what they were – big stone buildings with thick iron bars. [Possibly cattle sheds.] I remember we used to do the turnovers [mimes somersaults] on them bars. I don't know what they were. It just sticks in my mind. They were open fronted with these big iron bars. [Pause] I can't think what they were. And the grown ups were talking and laughing. Then us kids would be in bed. Talking and itching! All that straw poking in you. *Mrs AA*

After they'd finished their chores, some of the women would go to the pub, but this was not generally approved of. Just as the 'respectable' mothers would get their washing whitest, they would be the ones to disapprove of going to the pub during the week. The 'proper' mothers would wait until the weekend, when their men came from London to visit, before they ventured out to the local. The majority of the women agreed that it wasn't 'right' for married women to go to the pub without their menfolk.

Mrs M: Really, we made our own entertainment. Sitting outside the huts. Sit out there, you know. The children'd be in bed and we'd sit there till it got dark. Having a laugh and chatting.

G: Did you ever go to the pub during the week?

Mrs M: No, oh no. *Only* when the men came down visiting. That's all. In fact, everybody didn't go then, did they? Some of us women didn't go then. We was at home cooking the dinners. No only the men.

G: Did some of the women with children go to the pub during the week?

Mrs M: Oh yes. There were some rough ones. There were some rough ones. In fact I remember one year when we was at Whitbread's, there was a family came from Hastings, quite respectable people. So they used to go home at night. They were quite respectable people, see?

It wasn't only other women who didn't approve of mid-week visits to the pub, some of the children did not think much of the habit either. The children's disapproval seemed to result from resentment at being left out of the fun.

I used to have to go abed. And they used to all go out drinking! I used to get the right hump. *Mrs RR*

They'd go off and leave us in the hut! We was meant to be asleep, but we'd only pretend we was when they got back. *Mrs S*

It was not so unusual, or considered so unvirtuous, for the elderly female relatives to pay mid-week visits to the local. Perhaps this was because they no longer had so many child-care responsibilities or because different notions of respectability applied to grandmothers.

Mrs AA: The older ones always seemed to go down the pub. My young aunt'd be left in charge of us. But we'd sit in bed and talk. Make up our own games. My nan loved her drink. Stout and that, I think. But I know when she came back she'd get in bed and we'd go, 'Phew! Nan's been down the pub again.'

G: Did the women ever go down the pub by themselves in the week?

Mrs AA: No. Only the old grannies used to go. Have a walk

down there. Have their Guinness. It wasn't what the mums did. Not in the week.

The younger hoppers found other after-work pleasures and entertainments to occupy them in the evenings.

In the week the old girls, grannies and that, would go up and have a stout. *You'd*, the younger ones like, would go in the oast house where you dried the hops. Take up a big potato and the old boy'd put it in the ashes for you and cook it. [The 'old boy' here refers to the drier who would have to keep the hops turned to ensure even drying. He would sleep in the oast, in short snatches, constantly tending the hops, keeping an eye on how they were doing.] Yeh, then we'd have a singsong in there. It used to be really good. *Mrs AB*

But still the favourite evening pastime for the women was sitting together round the faggot fires, sharing tea, stories, songs and the company of their friends and temporary neighbours.

They was good times, sitting together, having a laugh round the fire. Good times. Always someone to have a chat and a laugh with. A bit of a singsong. You know. We'd all be there together, and we'd have the same sort of lives. So we'd understand one another, see? *Mrs S*

Mrs C: We used to sing the hopping songs sitting round the fire. 'When we go down hopping, hopping down in Kent,' and, er, 'They say that hopping's lousy, I don't believe it's true.' . . . Yes. Yes. There was all the different songs . . . There was the London songs as well, of course. 'Roll out the barrel,' and that! We'd all be there. All of us round the fire.

G: I bet you were tired out by the time you finally got to sit round the fire.

Mrs C: Yeh. It was good having the company but we was ready for bed, really.

G: Was it different at weekends?

Mrs C: Oh! Yeh! . . .

6
The Weekends

'And fun, and all!'

. . . You had to feed *them* and then go to the pub. Do your
shopping. Then start cooking again. Up the pub, home and
[laughing] bed! On Sunday, you got up, cooked the breakfast, some of the men went for a walk, ended up in the pub,
of course. *You* ended up in the pub about half hour before
shutting up time. And come back, wash up, and it was time
for them to go! *Mrs C*

By about midday on Saturday picking was usually finished for
the week. The women knew that they were expected to pick
enough hops to keep the drier, the oast house worker, supplied
for the rest of the weekend. Once that was done, the hoppers
would then be 'free' until Monday morning – free from their
paid work, at least. As in the evenings, there were still plenty of
jobs for the women to do at the weekends. The weekend chores
were a bit different though, they included the (usually pleasur-
able) job of getting ready for their visiting menfolk, as well as
looking after them once they'd arrived.

When trains were still the main form of transport to Kent, the
men who had remained back home in London would arrive
sometime on Saturday. Less often, they would get to the farm
on Friday night, but that was usually the time when the women

got ready for the weekend: cleaning up the huts, the children and themselves. If the hoppers were fortunate enough to be on a farm near one of the temporary bathing centres, set up by the missionary and other philanthropic societies, they could have a hot bath after work on Friday.

I remember all the men coming down at the weekend. We'd all have had a Salvation Army bath on the Friday to get ready. And be deloused at the same time if you was lucky! All before the men came down. Getting ourselves ready. *Mrs J*

But even if they couldn't benefit from having a Salvation Army sponsored 'penny bath on the common' the hoppers managed to prepare for their weekend visitors and the anticipated entertainment.

Washing yourself? You had a bowl outside. During the day we had rough old things on, but weekends we was all poshed up in our best. Out come the best didn't it? For our visitors! *Mrs M*

The visitors would also spend time preparing themselves for the weekend, making themselves presentable for their stay in the country.

This mate came down to visit us. All cased up in his suit! For the weekend. Down hopping in a suit! It was really funny how he was done up like! *Mrs D*

The children anticipated the arrival of the menfolk for reasons quite different from those of their mothers. They had other treats in mind. Mrs A's girlhood memories were quite different from the adult recollections like those of Mrs C above.

There was a great 'Hooray!' when all the men appeared, half sozzled most of them, but they were there. Saturday night

was *the* night. There were good things to eat and we'd have
been scrumping. We had a lot of food *and* a billy can of tea.
Some of them would even bring us pie mash down. A bit
bashed up by the time they got there but it was handsome!
And I know me nan had a stiff tipple. It was a jolly night.
[Laughing] *You* know.

Mrs M's husband spoke about his experience of being one of
the male visitors to the hop farms.

I didn't stop there, just that fortnight's pole pulling I told you
about, but I'd go down at weekends. Oh yeh. I wouldn't miss
that. We had some right old larks down hopping then.

The women remembered the fun and pleasure of the
weekends, but even then they had the continuous workload of
the household chores. The focus of the women's recollections
remained firmly rooted in the domestic even when talking
about their 'time off'. For instance, Mrs C described the scene
outside the Bull pub at Hunton:

Round there on the common on a Saturday night was like
being in a market in London. Lovely it was. All stalls. We
used to have a baker from Tower Bridge Road with the
bread. Used to come all the way down hopping. Another
man was there with the clothes. 'Tots' we called him. And the
butcher was there with his stall. On the corner. Friday night
and Saturday, and Sunday lunchtime. Really was a picture
round there.

Mrs AB also described the enterprising stall holders who
would come from London at weekends during the picking
season. She also reminisced about other diversions she associated with being 'down hopping'.

And fun and all! Specially over at Horsmonden. All round
the green at hopping time, you know, they used to have a

whelk stall, a sweet stall. The old umbrellas up over 'em. And on the Saturday nights they was there. Like a fairground it was. Yeh, used to be smashing. We used to have concerts in the village hall. Some dances, not a lot, mainly it was being together. Us like. Round the fire or down at the pub. Oh yeh, the weekends were special. Dad and all the boys would used to come down, see? So it was a right old booze up. We'd all be sitting outside on the green. Too many people to get inside the pub. [See Chapter 8 for a different version of why the hoppers sat outside.] It was smashing. Shilling on a glass. And shilling on a jug. I remember one night, our lot got pissed. Laugh! Oh dear! They come home singing 'Nelly Dean', and my brother had got hold of a bloody great umbrella. He was holding it out in front of him. He was soaked. We was *all* soaked. Another one of me brothers lost himself. Well, *we* lost me brother. All pissed . . . [Laugh]!

Walking back to the farm after the pubs were closed on a Saturday night was usually accompanied by a singsong. Some of the women suggested that this was to keep the groups together as they walked along the unfamiliar lanes, back to their huts. The lanes seemed very dark to Londoners used to street lighting. But, whatever the reason for their singing, it certainly gave a lot of fun and pleasure to the hop pickers and their visitors.

The pubs used to be full at weekends. You'd take your jug, they wouldn't trust you with the glasses. Some of the pubs'd charge a shilling on the glass though so you had something to drink out of! They were full at weekends. Jellied eel stalls and all that all round. The police didn't used to be able to get them out, so they'd get Joey Foot with his accordion and say, 'Play to 'em, Joey.' And they'd all march up the road. Just like the Pied Piper. It was lovely. My dad used to give me a flying angel. Right up on his shoulders he put me. And you used to get glow worms in the hedge in them days. He'd pick one up and put it on the front of his cap. 'That'll see us home,' he'd say. *Mrs J*

Mrs J told this story so vividly: the magical image of being led along the lanes by Joey Foot's music, following the light of a glow worm, it was hard to be sure that I hadn't been there too, sitting up on my dad's shoulders having a flying angel back to the huts. Glow worms were certainly found in the area at that time, the Natural History Museum verified this, but, rather unromantically, they doubted that Mrs J's dad would have seen much by his insect illumination. That seems a shame. Some of the male visitors got too drunk to benefit from even Joey Foot's musical guidance. The women talked about them regularly getting lost on the journey back to the huts, whether they had lights or not.

Shall I tell you what happened to D? Well, coming home from the pub, we got to this other farm. And he went in the hedge and we never saw him no more. He was drunk and he jumped the hedge. We never knew this at the time. Us crowd walking along, singing and laughing . . . He must have thought he was getting out to our farm but he had walked across the field and he was getting lost. So he stood in the field with his petrol lighter, just across the field, shouting out, 'Help! I'm lost.' The people all walking along said, 'Don't go near there, he might have a gun.' 'Cos you wouldn't know who was about. We didn't know it was *him*. I come home and went to bed and thought, 'Oh he's out there somewhere. Gossiping.' Instead of that he'd be lost in this field . . . The next day we heard the full story. Where he'd gone in the wrong direction . . . in the pitch dark, where there's a swamp. Standing there with a petrol lighter shouting, 'Help!' I'd have run a mile if I'd have seen him. I don't like the dark. *Mrs C*

All pissed! My mum was worried, she said, 'You'd better all go out and look for him.' She said, 'You don't know, he might have fell in the ditch.' Pitch dark! And there he was.

We found him. He's only cuddling a bleeding telegraph pole! He's saying, 'I never meant it love.' Silly sod. He'd had a fall out with the old girl. Yeh. Daft sod, cuddling the telegraph pole and saying he was sorry. And another night, me brother . . . he said to me other brother, 'I've lost me teeth.' Drunk again. So my brother gets up the next morning to look for the teeth and they was in his pocket. Yuch! . . . See, when they was bigger, me big brothers used to come down pole pulling, or they'd come down of a weekend. Like that time when he calls out to me mum, 'Mum, there's something licking my feet. It ain't half rough. Mum! It's horrible.' So, of course, Mum gets out of the other hop hut and goes to have a look. It was only a bleeding cow. Stuck its head in the hop house door licking his feet. What a treat licking his dirty feet! We've had some laughs with me brothers coming down of a weekend.
Mrs AB

Some of the men used improvised lighting effects to add to the general atmosphere of 'larking around'. Mrs D talked about her husband – an expert at getting laughs from his fireside audience.

Sung all the way home on a Saturday night, walking home from the pub we'd be. Coming along. Having a lark. Oh we had a laugh down there . . . Then we'd all sit round the fire and me husband'd go right down the bottom of the meadow. Creep away. And he'd light up a bit of methylated spirits. Up it'd go. Him pretending we had ghosts. All screaming and hollering, we was! Used to be lovely. Yeh, we always had a laugh. He always got us at it.

Mrs AB's brother didn't use quite such sophisticated props, but the effect of frightening the women into laughter was the same.

Old Annie went over the khasi. We was all back from the pub, having a singsong round the hopping fire. And old

Annie went over the khasi, and my brother saw her and thought, 'I'll frighten the life out of her.' 'Cos it was in the middle of the orchard, see. And he went over there with a sheet over him. So when she comes out of the loo. Didn't she scream! [All this was related with actions and voices to illustrate the story.] Awww my mum did grumble at him. She couldn't hit him, he was grown up. And he's stood there, like this, with the sheet pulled over him. [Laughing] Bloody fool!

When the adults and older children went into the village to the pubs, some of the younger ones, usually against their wishes, stayed behind at the farm. Mrs RR's father relented a little by telling her stories before he went off 'for his drink'. These didn't always have the effect of settling her down for sleep. The shadowy Kent nights were breeding grounds for bogeymen.

. . . at weekends there was all them who came down. All of them. And I can remember them going out. And there was no lights outside was there? Not like in London with the street lights and shops. And you used to have to walk through this wood. I used to have nightmares till they came in. I was only young but I was in charge of the other kids. All in the one hut together till they come back. See I wasn't frightened about being on me own, we was all together, but I used to think about them coming through this wood. Well you know what you're like when you're a kid. Your imagination runs away with you doesn't it? My dad used to tell you stories about this wood. And *then* they used to say you was daft being scared! All about ghosts he used to say. He'd tell you. [Pause] Some of the things he used to come out with, you know. He used to make me die. [Laughter] He always used to tell this: during the war, when he was in the jungle . . . And all the kids'd be sitting round the fire, mouths open . . . And he used to say he was going through this jungle and there'd be this snake. He'd have a snake in the story. Then there was *lions*! You know what kids 're like, we're all sitting there, believing it all. Then he said: 'This *tiger* come along. And it was a good job I said "Arsenal",' he said, "cos if I'd have said "Tottenham", that'd have been me lot!' He used to tell us that. Always. And we really believed it. This lion, tiger and Arsenal! My mum used to go, 'Oooooh!' 'cos he was right comical, my dad. But the stories he used to tell us about this wood. Then they used to go out and leave us in. Dear oh dear. [Pause] I used to sit thinking about it all. Yeh. [Pause] Think of 'em all coming home through there, the wood, after the pub'd shut.

Arsenal-supporting tigers weren't the only fantastic creatures of the night. 'Grey ladies' were often encountered in the dark lanes by Londoners on their way back from the pub. These apparitions were surprisingly constant in both gender and colour. Mrs C's daughter had an explanation for some of her mother's fears about these spectres:

Mrs ML: That old tree used to do you, Mum, didn't it? Looked just like a witch.

Mrs C: Yeh. With all them ghost stories, all the tales, all ones about the grey lady and that. [pause]

Mrs S: There'd always be a tree to frighten you.

Mrs ML: Yeh, but we had a grey lady. [Pause] Sat down there on the watershed.

Mrs C: That's right. She did. Down there on the watershed.

It was not only threats from supernatural sources that might worry the women at the weekends. When their men visited the farms there was always the threat of becoming pregnant, of having yet another 'hopping baby'.

Most of the babies born was May time. Every year see, the men came down at the weekends. And got drunk. *Mrs J*

My last one was a hopping baby. And I've got one April, one May, and the one June. *Mrs ML*

That was the husbands coming down of a weekend. *Mrs C*

We'd stay up late, enjoying ourselves, singing and dancing. You'd see the odd couple slope off down the fields and you'd say . . . [Silent gesture] *Mrs A*

Women with older daughters had an additional worry – that their girls might get 'involved' with the local boys. If they wanted to, however, the young women would always be able to find a way of meeting their lads, even when they faced the additional barrier of having their fathers staying for the weekend as Mrs AB did:

Course, when I eventually got in, my mum said, 'And where do you think you've been? You dad's going mad. You're late.' Well, with me being a young girl and out with all them boys around, see? She said, 'Where you been? Who you been with?' She said, 'Your cousin's been in a long time. She wasn't late.' And I said, 'I went for a walk.' And she said, 'Who with?' I said, 'A lovely fellah. He's got great big blue eyes, fair hair.' And my mum said, 'Yeh. And a brown arse!' And my mum *never* swore. My dad was going home the next morning. He said to me mum, 'Don't let her out tonight, mate.' I suppose they was worried about me.

The farmers saw socialising between the young local men and the 'hopping girls' from a very different perspective to that of the women. The farmers were, after all, locals, employers and men. One farmer I spoke to talked about the young men 'getting themselves hopping girls'.

In them days you'd get yourself a hopping girl. Them days, see, you'd pick for five or six weeks. Course the husbands and that . . . back in them days, they only 'seen' them of a

Saturday night. Then they'd go back again. That's where the old tale comes about hopping babies. When it came round to the next hopping they'd get another hopping baby again. That was quite [silent gesture] wasn't it, the thing? Getting yourself a hopping girl during the harvest time.

A publican who had served the hop pickers when the farms near his pub still had manual harvesting held similar views.

They all had babies born May time. Every year. See, the men came down at the weekend and got drunk. And some of them girls would like, get friendly with the locals. Some of them would.

The hop pickers certainly had a reputation for immorality and uncouth behaviour with some of the locals. This impression probably came partly from the overcrowded, shared conditions in which they were obliged to live.

Mrs RR: A little room with your bed in . . . that was the huts . . . the bed along the far end. You'd all have to muck in, boys and girls together.

Mrs T: Wasn't no room to 'muck about' though.

Mrs RR: No, course not. We just used to all sleep in together. Sharing the huts for sleeping. You're right. No bloody room to muck about!

The workers from the missions were not so sure that there wasn't 'room to muck about'. They worked vigilantly in their 'good fight' to combat what they saw as the hop pickers' immorality.

7
Religion, Missionaries and Social Control

'A slice of cake and the Hallelujah Chorus.'
(Leader of the League for Militant Atheism)

From the nineteenth century onwards many societies, from the Church of England Mission to Hop Pickers to various temperance groups, became involved in missionary work with the 'poor hoppers'. There are various written accounts of their efforts, often unintentionally hilarious in their sanctimony, which can be found in several books mentioned in the bibliography at the end of this book. This history was not intended to document their work, but the following extracts give an indication of their concerns. The examples are from 1892, 1933 and 1962, covering most of the period recalled by the women when they talked about their, and their families', experiences in Kent.

. . . the hopper was a most dangerous visitor – both sexes were alike feared. They were rebellious under the slightest restraints; notorious thieves; improvident in the extreme; lazy by day and riotous by night. But now owing to the advance of education, some are of the opinion – and greatly in consequence of the efforts made by Christian ladies and gentlemen to show them the better way of life – they exhibit a degree of improvement, which is both gratifying and important.

This 'rebellious' behaviour resulted, apparently, from the hoppers' untutored past:

> For years they were left to their own devices; and earning of money meant only the immediate gratification of their sensual passion . . . [they] squat upon the rich garden grounds of Kent in September. They have been turbulent and riotous, the evil infecting the good: they have been drunken and unmanageable; and they have occasionally destroyed the flowers they came to preserve. (Marsh, pp. 42, 47, 1892.)

> Indecent habits are common and open, and many a hitherto pure girl goes back to the city contaminated, to drift ultimately to the streets. (*Deliverer*, Salvation Army Magazine, 1892, cited in Bignell, p. 160.)

The hoppers were perceived as potential polluters of both the countryside and of virtuous maidenhood. But they could affect their patronising and patriarchal benefactors in yet other ways as the following extracts from Sargent show:

> It teaches us what are the real values . . . But it hurts as well. The needless suffering; the pathetic attempts to fight overwhelming odds; the rage response to kindness and encouragement; the simplicity of the outlook; the lack of deviousness; the loyalty of wives to unworthy husbands; the pride of the fathers in their children; the lack of self-control, so slightly beneath the surface; the pathetic finery – all go to make our hearts ache, because, at the best, we can do but so very little . . .

He continues with this 'improving' anecdote:

> I heard only the other day of a leader of the League of Militant Atheism who sneered at all the relief works and referred to them as 'A slice of cake and the Hallelujah Chorus.' He spoke most bitterly and contemptuously of

works such as our mission and stigmatised them all as efforts on the part of the class church to keep people quiet . . . [But] A picker, a man to whom I was talking one day, said that he preferred Christianity to Communisim (as he saw it in London) because Christians *did* things, whereas 'bolshies' (as he called them) were all talk.

'Distressingly', for him, some souls were beyond help:

On the other hand, a stranger woman who had more drink than was good for her came down to the mission and started blackguarding us, and me in particular because I wouldn't open the canteen during the staff rest hour, and said, 'I suppose you think you are a lot of b. . . .y [sic] toffs come down to patronise the scum!'

He concludes, somewhat surprisingly:

So there are two points of view. Be that as it may, our people are our real friends, and they trust us and we them, and our life together is perfectly happy; for it is not based on politics nor on social class, nor anything as transitory as that. It is based on love. (Sargent, pp. 100–102, 1933.)

Other missionaries who went to the Kent hop gardens reflected on their effect on their temporary flock of black sheep. They usually arrived at comforting conclusions about themselves and their work. Spiritual job satisfaction was obviously an important factor in such work:

They were so many and we so few, and September so short that we could make little spiritual impression on them in the mass, but at least they recognised and with gratitude that the church was there because it cared. To the best of its ability it was trying to help them in the spirit of Bishop Frank Weston's words, 'Go out and look for Jesus in the ragged, in the naked, in the oppressed and sweated, in those who have lost hope, in those who are struggling to make good . . .' Doubtless we did our job very badly but some impression was made on the roughest and most uncouth which would bear fruit later on in making easier the ministrations of their parish priests at home. (Farley, p. 78, 1962.)

In 1961 an essay competition about hop picking was set by the West Kent Federation of Women's Institutes. The collected essays were published in 1981. The following extract is from an essay entitled 'Medical and Social Work'. In her essay, the writer Vera Thompson shows the same attitude – a combination of condescension and Christian concern – seen in the earlier works quoted above.

Many of the visiting hoppers were lawless and vicious, the scum of London's East End, and good-intentioned people going among them to help were submitted to insults and abuse. Even where good accommodation was provided it was soon reduced to a shambles. The standard of morality is illustrated by the custom of 'hopper marriages'. An extempore 'priest' would mumble a few words over the joined hands of a pair, who had then run hand-in-hand to jump over a hop pole held by 'bridesmaids' and their young men. These unions rarely lasted after picking.

She continues in this same morally-panicked tone, using documentary evidence to support her misgivings about the hoppers' behaviour:

Drunkenness was another problem, and this was aired in the correspondence columns of *The Times* in September, 1881: 'How is it possible that in a country which is not only professedly Christian, but considers itself competent to send out missionaries to other countries, the high street of a considerable County town [Maidstone] can be thronged with drunken men and women, and the side streets and alleys blocked with human beings prostrate with drink . . . Meanwhile the whole rural population in the hop-cultivating districts of Kent is demoralised, not only in the matter of drink.' Another correspondent added: 'The society is fatally promiscuous . . . Mothers come back drunkards or immoral; daughters, even at 14 or 15 years of age, debauched and ready for the streets, and little children glib tongued in obscenity and blasphemy.'

Vera Thompson then cites the workers, the moral cavalry, who came to the rescue:

There were people who were alive to these conditions already at work in the hop gardens. Their sole resources faith and love of humanity, they nevertheless made their mark and the areas in which they worked began to improve . . . In 1930 . . . the Hop Pickers' Medical Treatment Board [was developed] with representation from [the] pioneer organisations . . . The work goes on but the end is in sight.

Despite their class assumptions, prejudice and paternalism, the missions were admired by many hoppers who recognised that they provided a mixture of spiritual and physical facilities for their benefit. Their efforts ranged from a local vicar reading uplifting texts outside the huts on Sunday mornings, to the creches organised on the largest farms by the Salvation Army. It can be imagined that some of the facilities were more widely appreciated than others.

Father Richard Wilson of St Augustine's in Stepney received widespread approval for his work which eventually resulted in his setting up the Little Hoppers' Hospital at Five Oak Green. He had determined to do this after coming face-to-face with the reality of poverty which denied even basic health care to some of the hop pickers. (Another situation which, like the destruction of dock workers' rights discussed in the introduction, seems to have worryingly contemporary resonance). The particular

We went to London Bridge to catch the train about four in the morning. All hop pickers special trains. *Hulton Picture Company*

Some places used to have them galvanised tin huts . . . Bit cut out of the top of the door – and that was it! Your light and ventilation.

Hulton Picture Company

You was all in it together . . . You didn't live in each other's pockets but you was close. *Museum of Kent Rural Life*

You got away from that being
'cramped in', in London.
Once you got out in the fields
it was so different . . . We
never had no holiday, never,
apart from hopping.
Maidstone Museum

I think to myself: it was a *hard way of living*, for what you earned for what you done. And the hours you put at it.
Maidstone Museum

Used to bundle all the kids
up and take them with you,
didn't you? When you was on
the field everybody seemed to
be watching together.

It wasn't hard work, but it was tiring. And the bines was really rough. You used to get scratched. *Maidstone Museum*

The Salvation Army ... they used to make tea and all. They was doing their best to get us teetotal! Keep us off the beer. *Hulton Picture Company*

top
Corned beef stew, sausage
stew. Bit of boiled bacon. Nothing
elaborate. Whatever would go in the
hopping pot. *Rita Game*

bottom
And how about eating
sandwiches with your hoppy
hands? Lovely, make 'em
taste better. Make the cheese
and onion taste all the better!
Hulton Picture Company

The men was pole
pullers . . . The pole pulling
was more money 'cos it was
men's work. When they
weren't drinking. *Hulton
Picture Company*

It's always been the women
who did the picking. The
only time we had men
picking was in the thirties.
When they was all on the
unemployed. *Hulton Picture
Company*

Nan always took her
washboard. And a big tub.
Used to fill it with cold water
and hot water'd be poured on
from the fire. Hang it on
lines from one hut to another.
And that washing was *always*
clean . . . Pure white. *Hulton
Picture Company*

Now when I think how hard my nan had to work. To me it was just a big adventure . . . Me poor old nan. *Museum of Kent Rural Life*

Washing yourself? You had a
bowl outside. During the day
we had rough old things on,
but weekends we was all
poshed up in our best. *Hulton
Picture Company*

There was a great hooray when all the men appeared . . . at the weekend. You had to feed them and then go to the pub. Do your shopping. Then start cooking again. Oh yeh! The weekends were special. Round the fire or down at the pub. *Hulton Picture Company*

Rita Game

With all the fields and people
around me, all sharing
together . . . I was 'me' when I
was there . . . I can smell the
hops and I can see it all.
Wasn't it lovely! *Gilda O'Neill*

shocking instance that had spurred Father Wilson into providing medical care for the poverty stricken pickers was the
occasion of his meeting a woman carrying a brown paper parcel
which he discovered was her baby. The mother had carried her
infant the five miles from the hop fields to a doctor, wrapped in
paper to keep it warm, only to be told that it was dead. The
Little Hoppers' Hospital provided an invaluable and genuinely
respected service for many years. It dealt with everything from
minor ailments suffered by the children to the horrific injuries
which occurred on the farms and in the sheds housing the
hop-picking machinery.

The 'real' job of the spiritual workforce, however, was seen
by many of its exponents as being essentially concerned with the
souls of the hoppers. Most missionaries quickly realised that
their religious endeavours would be far more popular if they
also offered practical benefits to their congregation.

G: Did your farm have the vicar come round?

Mrs D: Yeh. That's right. And the Salvation Army. They
used to have a place there, penny bath on a Friday. The
Salvation Army. In Yalding they had a proper place but *they*
had this big tent they'd bring and put baths in it. Penny a bath
on a Friday night. [Laughing] They'd be hoping to improve
you at the same time.

G: What if someone got ill down there, who would you send
for?

Mrs D: Well if you was in Yalding, you used to be able to go
to the Salvation Army, 'cos they was like nurses, wasn't they?
Used to come round every day anyway, didn't she? Of a
night. She used to holler out, 'Anybody want anything?' The
kids all used to go for a dab of ointment or whatever.

G: Spoon of malt.

Mrs D: That's right. They done a lot of work, the Salvation
Army. Salvation Army was marvellous in Yalding. Really

marvellous. They was the ones with the penny baths, wasn't they?

In keeping with their convictions the Salvation Army did their best to temper the amount of alcohol drunk by the hoppers, hoping that some would see the light and sign the pledge. They offered what they hoped were tempting alternatives to the jugs of beer which had traditionally been available during the working day in the fields.

Mrs D: They came round with tea and cake round the hop garden. Penny a bit. With a big bag. She'd holler out, [posh voice] 'Tea–O, Cake–O.'

G: They were all a bit posh were they?

Mrs D: Oh yeh. They all had money. You see they did good work. They did. They was the ones who could afford to do good work, you see.

Not all the women were keen to associate with the mission workers. Mrs T, for instance, had a real mistrust of the Salvation Army, which she claimed resulted from an earlier experience with a religious organisation based in London:

Sally Army? Yeh. Everyone used to run to their huts to get away from them. [Laughing] We knew all about them from what we called the 'Peculiar Church' down Canning Town. You used to get a sweet if you went. So we all marched up there, this Wednesday, and sat down. You can imagine us, can't you? So he said, 'Right, we'll start the service.' So we all looked at each other. And he said. 'I'm very sorry, there's no sweets.' You never seen a hall empty so quick in your life. He lied!

If the hoppers did decide to participate in the pious activities offered by those usually sincere people, it was not always with the spirit of reverence which had perhaps been hoped for.

Saturday night they'd get all the kids sitting in a ring round the fire singing hymns. They'd try and get the grown ups to join in. They'd all be so drunk. So they'd join in. Singing rude songs, not the proper words. *Mrs S*

We had Mr Feltham come round. A bible puncher. You know. Used to have all the kids round him singing. And used to have a concert of a night. And when it was raining, the mud! And all the kids used to get round him and sing, 'Bless the Lord, Bless the Lord, We don't know shit from clay.' Awww! My mum used to say, 'Hark at them kids.' Aw dear. 'Bless the Lord, Bless the Lord, We don't know shit from clay!' *Mrs AB*

The Reverend F. J. Feltham was a well-known figure around the Horsmonden area of Kent. It might not seem so from the quote above, but he was appreciated by many pickers for his earnest efforts to improve their conditions of employment and their welfare. He mounted a series of successful campaigns, for example, in getting hoppers' special trains running at a reasonable time in the morning rather than at night. But such triumphs failed to impress Mrs AB:

I was going across Horsmonden Green to a hoppers' concert put on by the sky pilot, you know him . . . So, we got to this bleeding concert, and there's this tart singing, [mock soprano] 'Oh the birds in the trees.' Christ! You should have *heard* it. So I said, 'I've had enough of this!' And we buggered off!

Mrs AA was slightly more willing to sample the entertainment offered by the spiritually-inspired musicians, even though her feelings were a bit contradictory.

Mrs AA: We had the Sally Army . . . they'd be playing away. And we didn't know the words to all the church songs, 'cos we weren't really churchy. But we'd sing along. It was a different atmosphere. You'd get down there, all Londoners, you know, all your own codes of living – and the ways you talk, the ways you sing – they're all different to other ways. Then you get these ★★★★★-type people Oh! [Laughing] Oh! leave that out, Gilda! You know I meant *country* with a *rrrrrr*! Oh mind you, I think I was right the first time!

G: I'll leave it out, A! [Laughter] I think I'll have to censor this, what with the bad language and you naked in Wellington boots! [A reference to a story Mrs AA had told me earlier.]

Mrs AA: [Laughing] The *countryish* type people with their banjos and their trumpets. It was something so different. We'd seen it in London on the street corners of a Sunday, but down there, it was something different.

The mockery must be seen in the context of the women's mostly very fond acknowledgment of the services that they felt the missions had provided. For all her criticisms of the 'sky pilot' and his singing 'tart', Mrs AB valued *some* of the work done by him on the hoppers' behalf:

This bloke I was talking about, well, he came from London. Mr Feltham. And I'll tell you what he did. Well, if anyone hurt themselves they had a medical mission. It was that sort of thing that was good. That was good. *Mrs AB*

But even when the missionaries' work was valued, women like Mrs D, quoted at the beginning of this chapter, were obviously very aware of the ulterior, if worthy, motives of their charitable helpers. The women would have become accustomed to their work through the missionary societies' bases in east London.

G: Did you get the Salvation Army round by you?

Mrs C: Yeh. Yeh. They used to bath the kids for a penny on Bull Common. [The open area outside the Bull pub.] There'd be the bath on the grass, but covers round it, like a tent.

Mrs S: And they did the delousing. [Wrinkling her nose in disgust at the idea.]

Mrs C: And they had a medical hut there.

G: Was that the Medical Mission?

Mrs C: No, the Salvation Army. And they used to show films over at the farm. And they used to cook big cauldrons of puddings of rice and come round the hop gardens with it. Ha'penny and a penny a serving. Well, they'd all have some. They used to make tea and all. More so when we'd have our dinnertime. On the common [the open area on which the huts were sited] they'd do it. Have it there for us all to have some.

Mrs S: They was doing their best to get us teetotal! Keep us off the beer.

Mrs C: That's right! That's what it was actually for.

Mrs S: I prefer a cup of tea any day. But they didn't know that. Thought we was all after the beer!

The mission workers might have been surprised to find that their services were not always utilised in the same generous spirit in which they had been offered. Mrs ML, for instance, used the visiting missionary worker as a disciplinary weapon when dealing with difficult younger members of the family.

Mrs ML: How old's our T? [Her daughter] Well, when she was about four she used to call them the 'carbuncle ladies'.

Mrs C: And that was all because her grandad had a carbuncle and they used to come over to the hut and dress it for him.

Mrs ML used to say, 'If you don't behave yourself the nurse'll take you away.' And T used to say, 'No! Not the carbuncle ladies!' That was the nurses from the mission.

It is illuminating to compare the attitudes of the missionary workers towards the hop pickers with the relationship between the pickers and the local Kent people. Notions of cockney immorality and the view that the Londoners were a people apart, 'not at all like nice people like us' were commonly held. This relationship between the 'foreigners' and the 'home dwellers' is the subject of the next chapter.

8
Us and Them: Relationships with the Locals

'Dirty foreigners.'

Estimates vary as to how many 'foreigners' went to Kent during the hop-picking seasons, when hand harvesting was still the favoured method. The available evidence suggests that anything up to a quarter of a million people is a reasonable assumption. The pickers must have gone to Kent in their tens of thousands at least, as some large, individual farms would each have employed several thousand temporary workers every year. The crucial consideration here though is not the actual numbers involved, but the impact that such an influx of city dwellers had on small rural communities, and the effects of this influx on relationships between the two groups.

As with any memories, time and present-day anxieties can act as filtering processes, allowing the recreation of 'going down hopping' as a golden age to be longed for, a time to be missed. A nostalgic idealisation of hop picking can gloss over the hostility and resentment felt by locals when confronted by the annual 'invasion' of Londoners. Morsels of evidence for this did occasionally surface in the women's memories, tempting in their strangeness and telling different stories to those which I, and others, remember so fondly. Clues pointed to the local people's prejudices which had become entrenched as 'truths' about the dirty pickers, their immorality and their uncontrolled lives. These versions of the past came so close to the stereo-typical beliefs of the morally-righteous missionaries that, at times, I wanted to despair. Perhaps I was naive, but I was shocked to find that people found outsiders a threat just because they were outsiders. I was one of those outsiders, but I don't remember feeling a threat to the moral fibre of the Kent countryside – perhaps I never noticed.

Nostalgia works in more ways than one; it can comfort, yes, but it can also hide the lived experience of people who do not have access to the mechanisms of denial. While I was resear-ching this chapter I happened to see the following 'and finally' human interest item featured on an ITN six o'clock news broadcast (24 September 1985). It told the story of three elderly women who had been hop picking since girlhood, until their farm had finished manual harvesting. The three women were shown revisiting the Kent hop gardens. The difference between this and their previous visits was that this time they were 'going down in style'. The film showed them sitting in the back seat of a chauffeur-driven Rolls Royce, and then standing around a bin, stripping hops from a bine in an otherwise empty field. They were filmed walking around the farm where they used to be employed, part of which has now been converted by Whitbreads into a hop museum. The location then changed to show a full-screen shot of the outside of the Bell pub, a Whitbread house of course, which stands opposite the museum. The viewers were then shown inside the pub, a show-piece for the brewery, all rustic charm, country artefacts and draped hop bines. The women sat in plush chairs, drinking happily and smiling at the camera, 'just like they used to'. Memories had been sanitised; the myth of 'the good old days' was complete.

During my work researching the background for this book, I went to the Whitbread museum, where I met the Leisure Manager, Peter Lesley. Mr Lesley had himself managed a hop farm. He organised a courier to take me round the exhibits, instructing her to tell me all about the huts and the pickers. He was very helpful, and apparently enjoyed the opportunity to talk about his work, but he became embarrassed, as did the courier, when I mentioned after the tour that I had been taken picking when young. He hurried to assure me that as a child he had known a family who had been 'the salt of the earth', and they had been pickers too. They were 'genuine people', he explained, and could even be classed as 'respectable', they 'didn't have much' but . . .

The following remarks were made by the courier as she showed me around the hop museum (15 May 1985):

The last hand pickers were here in 1968. The Medway flash floods provided a good opportunity to get rid of them. There were such bad relationships with the village, it was becoming impossible for us. They were so anti-pickers, the locals. The Bell [the pub shown in the news item] would pretend to close during picking. Locals drank secretly in its kitchen, going in the other way. They didn't want the pickers. They were really anti-pickers. Funny how people only remember the good bits. I have old ladies come here who cry when they come in here. [We were standing in an oast house which houses part of the museum's collection.] People had children christened and even got married by the vicar down here. Hopping was so important to them. Someone told me about one old lady who even had 'Pull No More Bines' put on her gravestone. Whitbread's were known for their high standards – good huts, entertainments, treated well – regular pickers were really glad to get on to Whitbread's farm. There was even our own shop.

The courier continued speaking throughout the tour of the farm. She pointed out to me a whitewashed square on the outside of a brick farm building.

That was where the films were shown on a Saturday night. It kept some of the pickers away from the village pubs. We did our best, but there was no stopping some of them.

The hoppers were well aware of some of the controls being

exerted by the local people. There were various methods of keeping them either out of the local pubs, or at least from exercising their 'dishonest' city ways.

A lot of them didn't like us. All right through here it used to be. They never used to actually close the pubs in Yalding though. But always a shilling on the glass if you wanted a glass of beer, wasn't it? Wouldn't even let you have a glass of beer without the shilling deposit! *Mrs D*

Signs saying 'No pickers' were clearly displayed on the doors of many pubs. Some would only have the sign on the door to the lounge or the select bar, allowing the pickers entrance into the public bar. Others would serve the pickers through a window, allowing them to sit outside, keeping them segregated from the locals inside.

Mrs C: Shilling on a glass, and you wasn't allowed in the locals' bar. You was only allowed in the public bar. And from there they'd go round and serve you through a little window out the back. That's what used to happen at the Bull. The locals only were allowed in round the front.

Mrs S: Saloon bars were for the locals only, you see. Not for us.

Mrs ML: Public bar *if* you was lucky.

Signs saying 'No gypsies' were enforced most rigorously; travelling people were rarely welcomed into any of the bars. The travellers were seen as a particular threat, an uncontrollable group to be feared. 'Foreigners' and 'home dwellers' alike had their views on such families. Some people spoke about violence and revenge attacks between gypsy families. Mrs AB talked about a row developing between two families as to who was entitled to a farmer's 'twiddling' work. Twiddling is the essential work carried out early in the growing season which involves training the young hop shoots around the stringing. On many farms, it was accepted that a particular family traditionally got the work as part of their yearly cycle of employment tied to the growing and harvesting seasons.

Us Londoners wasn't that bad, but over where you'd get them travellers. You know. The rows between all them big families! . . . They'd be buying and selling their horses on the green, and there'd always be a bloody fight. *Always*. They'd have to close the pubs. Not have them open . . . Even some of the better parts, they'd have to close the pubs. There was even a shooting. Someone got killed over a row about who was doing some twiddling work on one of the farms. Shot him he did. Just like that. No wonder they closed the pubs! *Mrs AB*

The pub owners and managers must have faced a real dilemma: the availability of all that custom, particularly at weekends, weighed against the risk of offending the regular customers by requiring them to mix with such 'undesirables'. Yet those regular customers might themselves be making money out of the 'foreigners'. The regular customers would have included the shopkeepers, trades-people and the farmers themselves – they, at least, must have shared the publicans' ambivalent attitude towards the hoppers.

The shopkeepers dealt with potential thieves by covering their shelves and displays with chicken wire. The goods could be seen but not touched. Another tactic was to hand the purchases through a window, or hatch, similar to the pubs' system of control – allowing hoppers to buy but not to enter the premises. The owners who did allow hoppers into their shops were cautious enough to ensure that their numbers were strictly limited.

The shops had the chicken wire up. Like a bar wasn't it? To stop you. Wired across. They didn't trust the Londoners, that's why. Anything went missing! They just didn't trust you, let's be honest . . . They'd talk to you and that, but I think it was the shopkeepers mostly that were suspicious . . .

they got flustered when the shop got more crowded than they allowed. *Mrs C*

Used to have this shop . . . they used to queue right back! You couldn't imagine it. And she used to let them in a few at a time. And there was Mrs R who used to serve the bread pudding and that through her own window! Make it herself and sell it through her window! *Mrs AB*

They used to make us line up outside, then they'd call us in one at a time. Like they do now in the sweet shops round our way. With the school kids. *Mrs S*

The sweet shops that Mrs S was talking about are in the East End of London, but they are not the only shops still to practise such security methods. I was told by a museum curator who lives in Kent that wire barriers, protecting the goods, have recently been erected in some of his local shops. The potential thieves now feared, however, are not hop pickers but foreigners of a different kind – French day trippers on the ferries from Calais and Boulogne!

Mrs B had owned a general shop from which she had served the hop pickers for many happy years. She serves as an important reminder that not all locals saw the pickers as criminals, or as spreaders of immorality, as might have been construed from the caution exercised by some publicans, shop-keepers and missionaries:

G: Was it good for trade when the Londoners were here?

Mrs B: Oh yes. Then it was. It was all right then.

G: Did you have any problems?

Mrs B: Oh no. They were different sorts of pickers who caused trouble. We were lucky. The ones who came down here were all right.

G: Where my family went picking, round Laddingford, they

used to put chicken wire cages all over the stuff to stop us pinching it.

Mrs B: Oh yes, that wasn't unusual. It's very *nice* out there in Laddingford, you see. We never had to do anything like that . . . There were some rough ones. We all knew that.

G: Apart from the increase in trade, what else did it mean when the hoppers came? What was it like?

Mrs B: It used to be fun. The young people especially used to like it. There'd be a singsong round the pubs, all that sort of thing.

G: Did the pubs round here let the pickers in?

Mrs B: Our one, our local, the Hop Bine, was always pleased to open to them all, wasn't it? Almost exactly the same faces. Year after year. Yes, the same. As a matter of fact you used really to look forward to seeing them. Well, yes, glad to see a bit of life. It was certainly brighter. Jolly . . . The friendliness. My shop was lovely for me . . . There was this little shop in Rotherhithe that my mum had when I was 10 or 11. Well then I served in that shop . . . so I could serve in my one, down hopping!

G: So running a shop was a skill you already had then?

Mrs B: Yes! I've also worked in Woolworths as a girl. You know I really liked that work down hopping. Meeting them people . . . Used to be smashing with them hop pickers, didn't it?

The idea that there were different kinds of pickers – rough and respectable – was supported by locals and Londoners alike. The pickers, for instance, were clear about what was unacceptable behaviour: going to the pub in the evenings without the men; the gypsy families' fights; badly-washed 'whites', and so on. Farmer D was concerned about the behaviour of 'his' pickers in a paternalistic way, reminiscent of feudal relationships between squire and peasant.

We had our regulars. Been coming down here for years, and their mothers and their parents before them. And the girls have carried it on. We've never had no bother. We used to have a few fights, amongst themselves, but we used to get on pretty good. We used to play the next farm down at football matches. Sundays. H's and M's farms. Have return matches, 'cos they was full of hop pickers. *All* Londoners. We never had nothing, being a small farm you've got them under control, see? But there's some rough people used to come down here, you know. But not ours. We'd keep ours pretty well sorted out. Being smaller we could keep more control over them. You get a thousand London families on a place, you know what they was. I mean all them East Enders! Taking knives. There'd be fights. You know what the East End was like. Not that it's a lot better now. There's so much violence there now. We used to have apple minders in them days 'cos of the scrumping. Used to have blokes mind the orchards from the grown ups, not so much the kids! They'd have odd arguments over the girls. Well they used to call us, what was it? 'Country bumpkins.' And now what did we call them? Got some nickname for them. Cockney somethings. We had to have mounted police down the local pub at weekends to keep the people in order. Wouldn't believe that now, would you? How quiet it is now. But that's true. Mounted police. [Unless there was some sort of big event like a horse sale taking place, most areas would only have one or two additional police officers, known to the pickers as 'hopping coppers'.] And, of course, a lot of our pickers used to go to the Gypsy Fair at Horsmonden. All the fights. The gypsies was the cause of them. Once they got argumentative they never forgot old scores. So they meet again, somewhere like that, they bring it all up again. That's no good. Always avoid 'em, travellers and that. More damned nuisance than good.

Comparable views were voiced by ex-hop farm manager Peter Lesley, and also by representatives of English Hops Ltd, (the reformed Hop Marketing Board). The point made was that there were different types of pickers, and the bad ones had to be watched; control had to be kept in order to prevent trouble or feuds developing. It was also acknowledged that there were nicer types, the regulars on whom they could depend to do their work and behave properly:

> Well, when we was out there in the fields we used to laugh and sing all the old songs. One day the farmer came out and said, 'I've really enjoyed today.' And I said, 'Have you?' And he said, 'Yes. Hearing all you girls singing all those songs. I've really enjoyed it. It's a treat to see you all like this.' *Mrs AB*

It is probably an unfair, and certainly an unpleasant, comparison, but I couldn't help but be reminded of Hollywood films of the 1940s about farms in the 'deep south' of the USA which portrayed the exuberant workforce singing while they laboured for their master.

> *Mrs ML*: I was practically brought up in that farmhouse, wasn't I? The farmer's got two children David D and Sophia D and they called me Sarah D . . . anyone will tell you, I'm Sarah D. I still go over every Sunday now we've moved out this way and make Farmer his tea for him. Every Sunday.
>
> *Mrs C*: See it was only a small farm, and Mr D only a small farmer, but he was the lord and master, and that's it.
>
> *Mrs ML*: If I'm not there at four o'clock he phones me up and says, 'You're late.'

Mrs J had a more unusual perspective on this contradictory relationship between the locals and the cockney visitors. As a young woman she travelled with her family from their London home to pick hops. She then moved to Kent and continued to do some picking. She now runs a pub in the heart of the hop-growing countryside of Kent.

Now that I've been the landlady for ten years, I've sort of got the locals' confidence, and one of them told me that they used to pray for rain to wash the muck and filth away after the Londoners had gone home. Well! They made enough money out of the bleedin' Londoners! Like that shop in Hunton: used to cover all the shelves with chicken wire 'cos they didn't trust the Londoners. I don't know! Like we was all no good.

The women also said that the way the locals reacted towards them depended on whether they thought the pickers were rough or respectable types. But they also recalled the open prejudice with which they were sometimes confronted.

Mrs AB: Some of the old frumps *never* liked us Londoners. Londoners are different, they're more open-minded than this lot down here. No, if anything went wrong, it was the Londoners. Know what I mean? I've seen kids destroy that phone box before the Londoners have even got here, and I've heard 'em say, 'Oh well, the bloody Londoners are here.' So, of course, I've picked 'em up over it. Two or three people I've said to, 'Oh *no!* That was done by local kids. That wasn't Londoners at all.' Give a dog a bad name, that's it.

G: So, how about when you married a local man and moved here? When you picked then, were you a home dweller or a foreigner?

Mrs AB: Foreigner, still am! Yes and I've been living here 40 years now.

G: What did your husband's family think about him marrying a Londoner?

Mrs AB: Not a lot! Locals would turn their noses up at them going out properly with the hopping girls . . . and they was *so* nosey. Nosey. Put it that way. They'd be talking *to* you, and when you'd gone, they'd be talking *about* you. You see what I mean? They're not like us. I mean, with me, I'd go and have a row with someone, right? I'd be straight. Then if I see them in the street tomorrow I'd say 'Hello'. Well if they didn't answer me, I'd try again, and if they didn't answer me, I'd just think, 'Well, sod you.' But with them down there. They'd run from one to another, wouldn't they? And they'd all be adding a little bit to it. By the time it's all boiled down there's a proper old barney.

Mrs AB said that her mother had experienced very different, exceptional, reactions from the locals with whom she worked on the farm. She was very proud of the following story:

My mother was treated like a home dweller over Horsmonden. Yes, she used to go down their houses and that . . . As I say, Mum was treated like a home dweller. I never forget. She'd had a breakdown. Terrible. That wasn't at R's farm, but at P's when old Farmer C had it. She went there for 17 years, till they gave up hops . . . Well, poor old Mum had this breakdown. She'd come down but she was ill. The old bailiff came round and said to her, 'Mrs W,' you know how they talk, 'I want you to come out and do some work.' He said that would help her. She said, 'I don't want no work.' No, well she wasn't lazy. Well sure she wasn't with a family like that. But she said, 'I can't do that farm work, I don't know how.' They wasn't picking yet, see. He said, 'Come out and try.' See she'd really had a breakdown and come down for a couple of months. [Regular, trusted pickers would sometimes be allowed to use 'their' huts as holiday homes out of season.] So he got her out there on the farm. They really thought the world of her. He said, 'They're doing 'oeing,' She said, 'Gor blimey man, I'm living on the interest of what I owe now!' She did. I'll never forget it. She couldn't keep up, poor old girl, but they kept popping over to help her. So when the farmer come out he thought she was keeping up with the rest of the women. With the locals she was, and they was doing it for her. Yes, it's true.

Mrs AB's mother's treatment was not simply a matter of an earlier generation of Londoners having a better, more mutually respectful, relationship with the local people. The relationship which Mrs T describes below was between a member of her family and a local man. Mrs T's aunt was about the same age as Mrs AB's mother.

This aunt of mine, well she got 'into trouble' down there picking by a [pause] gentleman farmer. She went mad. Years ago. She was a young girl. Twenty. Went down picking. She went stark raving mad. Because when she took him to court, for the maintenance of *his* child. And he practically called her a prostitute. You know. Sent her mad and she died in the asylum. She had the baby, and when he [the child] found out what had happened, in later life, he committed suicide. He lived in the East End, they had their business there. His two children came home from school during their lunch hour, and he'd got his head in the gas oven. She'd died in that place. He used her and got away with it. *He* was a gentleman farmer, you know, a different class. Nobody'd believe her. They'd believe him . . . Just think, then, years ago, they'd stick you in a mental hospital if you'd had an illegitimate baby. Oh yeh. Even if they thought you was having sex with someone they could stick you in there . . . It was really dismal in there, my mum used to go and visit her. So they don't have to be in touch with the outside world. Keep them away from people on the outside. Terrible.

Such tragic events as those described by Mrs T may not have been the norm, but the attitudes and beliefs that could lead to the grotesque circumstances of the woman's and her son's deaths were not so unusual. Mrs AA eloquently summed up the barriers that could grow up between the East Enders and their temporary neighbours, resulting in the failure to understand each other's culture and values.

See, you're from London, so you're rough and ready and

you're gonna nick everything they've got. See, the grown ups, after they'd had a few drinks, might have been a bit loud, but not really any trouble. We'd fight with the local kids, that was the done thing. '*Dirty rotten Londoners.*' Wallop! But not any real trouble . . . The locals didn't always understand our ways. They thought we was brash and loud, always swearing. But we didn't always understand either. We'd get in trouble for damaging the trees when we went scrumping, but we didn't understand that we were doing damage. Just a few apples out of all them trees. We'd get a clip round the ear and be told not to do it again. '*Dirty foreigners.*' They probably wanted something to talk about, and that time of year they picked on the hoppers. *Mrs AA*

Mrs AB also had very definite views on why the locals and the East Enders sometimes failed to get on with each other. She believed that the local people lacked generosity, and that made them different to Londoners:

I'll tell you the truth of it, if they wasn't getting nothing out of it, they wouldn't give their shit to the crows. Too bloody mean. Wouldn't help anyone out if they could help it. *Mrs AB*

So divisions existed between the locals and the Londoners, and between the hoppers themselves. Perhaps such divisions will always exist between groups, causing splits and mistrust to occur, and even violence to erupt. When even one person chooses to be judgmental about another, labelling them as less worthy or dangerous, a victim must be found to bear that label of unworthiness or immorality. But there were also good things to remember – memories of friendships and kindnesses to be cherished by the women and their children.

9
The Importance of Being Together

'Because other than that, you're on your own.'

The pleasure and support the women found in the sharing of their daily lives with the other hoppers is a common theme in many of their reminiscences about the 'good old days'. The hop farm was a workplace where children could safely accompany their mothers and could even contribute their labour. An added, highly-valued advantage of working as a hop picker was actually sharing the care of the children. This benefit was spoken of frequently, and was favourably compared to having 'your family' around to help, but 'right there' in the workplace; like having the extended family or neighbourhood community that many of the women were part of back in the East End. As I did the interviewing I wondered if any of the women had experienced (as I had) the feeling of being a young, very new parent and desperately wanting to share all the strange, boring, mind-numbing chores with someone who felt the same. A 'network' it would be called now. I had not been able to find that sort of support, it didn't seem to exist for a newcomer in the small town to which I'd moved when I had my first child. The women who had moved away from their own families' communities confirmed that they felt very similar frustrations, and longed nostalgically for the support they would have got 'back home'. One of the usual reasons for moving away was, ironically, so that they could afford to set up in a home of their own. It is often when we have lost something that we learn to value it. The women's memories of the pleasures of communal life in the 'good old hopping days' certainly seem to confirm this.

Whole neighbourhoods of women and young children would transfer *en masse* from the East End to 'their' farm for hop picking. Having your own family, even your own neighbourhood, with you wasn't only comfortingly familiar, it could also mean that you would still be able to earn some money if you were ill. Regulations on the larger farms strictly stated that anyone who was sick would not be accepted for the season's hop picking. If the pickers fell ill while in Kent they would be sent home immediately. These rules were probably a hangover from the days when cholera and other epidemics had swept through the Kent hop farms. Outsiders were blamed for the diseases and for spreading them through the countryside.

Hoppers would do their best to make sure that the farmer was unaware of any sickness in 'their' communities. The women would cover up for friends, minding their children, even picking for them, to enable them to stay and earn some money to take home. The women talked proudly about the efforts made on behalf of friends and family.

The companionship of the other pickers was also highly prized by the women. Mrs J talked about the importance to her, as a young mother, of having the company of adults, and she spoke for all the women when she emphasised the relief of sharing the physical care of her children.

They were happy times, singing and laughing. I didn't like the picking, but it was the company. I went even though I didn't like the picking. The people, the atmosphere. You never had to look after your kids. My Michael! I used to have to tie a rope around him, like we used to do, tie him to the cookhouse. You know how they go, the kids, from bin to bin. When I couldn't find him I'd call out, 'Is Michael there? Is Michael there?' The call'd go right round the common.

They'd call bin to bin. Then he'd lose his 'bot bot'! He wouldn't sleep without that bot bot. Bloody old bottle. So the call'd go out, 'Anyone seen Michael's bot bot?' You'd find it in someone's hut, or someone's bin. Where he'd left it. We all looked after one another in them days. *Mrs J*

See, I knew my nan never had any worries when we was hopping. It was like a rest for her in some ways! Someone always knew where we were, see. All the so-called aunts. They wasn't me aunts, well, not all of them wasn't. Me nan could say, "Ere, where's A?' And someone'd say, 'She's all right, she's down here with mine.' The women could get on with their nattering, they'd not got the kids hanging around 'em. She knew we'd be all right. *Mrs AA*

Oh yeh, you'd mind anyone's kids. If you see them wandering too far, you'd call 'em back. Anyone's kids. *Mrs C*

The involvement of other people in the daily workload of caring must have been even more of a break from routine for women with larger than usual families. For mothers with sick and disabled children the sharing and support gave them respite from their constant responsibilities.

G: He was special to you, that little boy you looked after, Mrs D?

Mrs D: Yeh, that little boy. He was mental, and his mum used to have the bin next to me. And he was backward. And he, I don't know, he took to me. And he'd sit with me all day. And she took photos of us. He was 14 then but he didn't mature very well. But he was so backward, love him. But you could talk to him. I used to talk to him for hours. He liked that. He'd just sit by my bin.

G: He trusted you then?

Mrs D: Yeh, love him.

G: I bet it helped his mum, too.

Mrs D: I suppose it did. He took to me. All day he'd stay with me, by my bin.

It wasn't only child-care that the women shared, they also shared the few possessions that they had.

And like the kids'd all be looked after, you'd go with or stay with whoever, but always if someone *had* something, you'd share that and all. *Mrs RR*

See, you could earn with your children. Everybody kept an eye on other people's children. If they see them doing wrong or in trouble there was always somebody there . . . when you was on the field everybody seemed to be watching together, where the children all were. They were safe. They were more safe there than today. See, if anybody see you doing wrong, 'Hey!' Something like that, you know. Like a rest for women if they had lots of kids! . . . And if someone had something that'd do you, they'd let you have it . . . I was 'me' when I was there. With all the fields and people round me, all sharing together. Wasn't it lovely? *Mrs M*

Used to bundle all the kids up and take them with you, didn't you? Say, 'I'm taking her with me,' or 'You can take him up the field,' or 'How about with me?' 'All right then, go on!' All troop along of a morning. Together. We was all mates. We'd *all* share. If there was a jumble sale up the village, you'd buy bits for anybody. What you could get hold of. 'That'll do for *someone*.' Always the same. *Mrs D*

The impression given by the women in their stories was that the sharing of child-care, and anything else that they had or needed, came from an understanding of the poverty that they had all experienced. They might be the one in the fortunate position of being the provider or helper on one occasion. But that might be reversed the very next day.

You was all in it together. You knew about their troubles 'cos their lives was the same as yours. We was all like that. You know, helping out. *Mrs RR*

Even the children were taught to realise that there were times when they had to put the needs of others before their games.

It was friendly like. Everybody helped one another. Anybody was in trouble, there was always somebody there to help you out, and give a good word. If somebody was unwell there'd be food into them and that, before the others picked. My aunt'd take their kids, 'Come on, get picking,' she'd say to us, then us kids would stop and pick on the bins. To help them out, see? Make sure they'd get a bit of money. You looked out for one another, see. *Mrs M*

One year, Mrs AB's mother stayed on at the farm, after picking had finished, to help nurse another hopper's sick husband. Even though Mrs AB had 13 brothers and sisters, her mother still found the time and energy to help Mrs P.

. . . this boy, he was kicking a hedgehog round for a week – dead – and his father cooked it and ate it. Baked it. Well, he was really ill, see. We finished hop picking and by then he was ever so ill. So my mum said, 'I'll stop with you.' 'Cos his wife was frightened, see. My mum was only little but she had nerves of iron for anything like that. 'I'll stop here for a few days with you,' she said. 'Cos my mum could see he was on his way out. Well, anyway, then he had the rattles. And I'll *never* forget *that*. I was only a kid, but awwww! And he snuffed it in the end. So my mum said to her, 'That was that bloody hedgehog.' But she wouldn't have it. And he'd been playing football with it for a week, then he ate it! So they had this inquest up at the farmer's big house, at Horsmonden, up on the hill. So old C [the farmer] said, 'Give Mrs So and So [Mrs AB's mother] ten pounds for her trouble.' You know. My mum said, 'I don't want it.' She said, 'Give it to Mrs P.'

That was the widow's name. She hadn't helped out for no money. She give it to the widow. *Mrs AB*

When she reached adulthood, Mrs AB followed her mother's example of helping and supporting other women both in London and Kent. The 'services' she provided ranged from being an unofficial midwife to being the local expert at 'laying out' the dead relatives of friends and neighbours. Mrs AB's skills and assistance are still in demand. She had 'laid out' a neighbour's husband just a month before she spoke to me about her hop picking experiences.

Moving examples of mutual trust and care were woven throughout the women's memories. They told me many stories about help gladly given by the hoppers. The women who told the stories were on both the giving and the receiving ends of the help.

They'd come and help me, the people. They'd really help you. If I never had a shilling, they'd lend you one. If they had one! Wouldn't they? . . . And you'd be glad of the hand-me-down bits that they'd give you for the kids, wouldn't you. Especially if you had a load of kids. *Mrs D*

Mrs D wasn't the only grateful recipient of secondhand clothes for her children. Mrs AA wasn't sure where her new things came from when she was taken to Kent, but she guessed, and she knew that her grandmother was pleased to get them for her.

I always remember Nan used to be really chuffed when she come up with these 'new' clothes we never took with us. I couldn't exactly say where she got them [laughter] . . . I think they used to be the bits theirs'd grown out of, and passed it on. And someone else'd pass *their* bits on.

The women also supported each other in less tangible but equally important ways. The following quote was part of an interview with a woman who was beaten, with horrible regularity, by her husband.

> It was a community feeling . . . you could chat to Mrs D and you could chat to Mrs L or whatever . . . you didn't live in each other's pockets but you was close. You could sit and say, 'Well my old man beat me up last night.' Or this or that. You could talk to them people, knowing that they was feeling the same sorts of feelings that you was feeling. You could turn to one another. The friendliness – that was good. Made you feel better.

The 'people', 'community' and 'friendliness' were mentioned time and again as being the most important things that hopping meant to the women. 'We was all one' was a phrase which recurred in the interviews. When I asked what was the most valued of all their experiences 'down hopping', several women replied, 'We was all one.' The expression also featured in a television programme of the same name that my parents remembered seeing. The film was about Londoners and the 'old days'. I asked the women who used the phrase if they had seen the film, wondering if they had picked it up from the television. Apart from the two women who had actually been in the film, it was unfamiliar to them. They all expressed a great interest in it, however, welcoming an opportunity to be reminded of the closeness they all valued so highly.

> It was always like that. Always the same families. Some'd come from Stepney, some'd come from Canning Town, some from Bow. Some'd come from Custom House, wouldn't they? You'd meet them all there. 'Hello! How are you?' All the old mates. The best thing about it, I think, the people. The friendliness, and the people. Soon as you arrived they used to holler out, 'Got the kettle on. You get your beds made up.' You don't get people like 'em today. *Mrs D*

> See it was the time for people to get together. The time of our

lives when *everybody* got together. That's important you see.
Mrs R

We'd all be there. All in it together. You knew your
neighbours in them days. Most of 'em would be down
hopping with you anyway! Off we'd all go. *Mrs S*

Mrs T was another one of the women who remembered the
hop picking community as being a simple geographical transfer
of the East End community in which she lived during the rest of
the year.

We all came from one road in Canning Town, where all the
trams used to run through. We all came from there. All down
the same road . . . It was a very close-knit community, and
you was all in the same boat. Nobody was better than
anybody else. *Mrs T*.

The fond memories were qualified by Mrs C. In her descrip-
tion of what hopping meant to her, she returned to the idea that
there were always some people who would act badly, showing
up the rest of the hoppers. Hers was not a superficially
romanticised view of the past.

I would say hopping was a very enjoyable part of my life . . .
I'm not saying I had a rough life, don't get me wrong, but to
go down hopping, then to go home, I'd think, 'Oh! Tonight
I'd be round the Bull.' I'd miss it. You know. And all the
people'd be there. Or if it was a lovely day, 'We'd be up the
field picking,' I'd think. You know, honestly, that is [pause] I
would say the people were important to you *when* they're
amicable. Which they were. [Pause] As long as they didn't
quarrel I was all right. And if they were singing, I was all
right. But if they were quarrelling, which some people do in
drink, don't they? [Pause] Then I wasn't all right. They could
be a right show up, some of them. Get us all a bad name, the
way they carried on. But it was a community life really. We

all shared. Good and bad. I think it was very important, because other than that, you're on your own. *Mrs C*

I talked to the other women about Mrs C's point that some hoppers didn't know how to behave, and how they could 'get us all a bad name'. Just as the women had described the locals' responses to them as being dependent on whether they were classed as 'rough' or 'respectable', they acknowledged that their own relationships with the other hoppers were similarly affected. Certain 'types' were not approved of at all. The disapproval resulted from a variety of proscribed behaviours, from being a 'bad' mother, to generally behaving 'improperly'. The list of the unacceptable depended on agreed notions of propriety – poverty did not have to mean a lack of virtue.

She was a wicked cow. Used to whack them kids with a stripped bine. My mum used to have a right go at her. 'You leave them kids alone, or I'll sort you out!' she used to say. A wicked cow she was. *Mrs S*

I mean, the way they'd sit there. Sun tops and swimming costumes. It wasn't the place for swimming costumes. It wasn't the place for that. And I'm sure that if half of them knew what a sight they looked . . . Terrible behaviour. *Mrs C*

Used to have an ice cream van call on the common . . . One of the women run out to him in her drawers and bra. *He* never came back. *Mrs ML*

There were also 'types' who, it was understood, should best be avoided if the women were not to be seen as guilty by association. It was generally agreed that they were the worst of all.

There were different types of pickers. I mean you'd get some of them slopping along in their old man's cap on their head. I mean. Awww! Ours was a respectable family. That's right.

Well, if my mum used to see my sister-in-law's mum, she used to dodge her, if she could. Didn't want to be seen with the likes of *her!* No thank you. As I say, she used to wear her old man's cap and a pair of bleeding boots with no laces. Well, it shows us Londoners up, that do. Doesn't it? Yes, it does. And that rough one, that Ada. I remember *her*. Some of them gave Londoners a bad name. That Ada. She used to go to the pub, come back *paralytic*, really pissed. They used to have to go and bring her back. Awww! She was a disgrace. She was a right Tower-Bridge-Roadite. Sort of erratic. Common. You know. The way she used to behave. I don't know what happened to her. But that's the trouble, isn't it? Give one or two of them a bad name. 'All them Londoners', this and that. We all like a drink, but get pissed? Show yourself up like that Ada behaved? Had a terrible name. You all knew what was going on. Everyone did. *Mrs A B*

Ada didn't manage it, but the women all knew that it was possible, even admirable, to be 'properly behaved' even if you didn't have much. How you behaved was the most important thing, and that depended on a proper upbringing.

You'd be classed as common. Well, you were common *anyway*. You were lower, low down, if you went hopping. But we always come, from kids. And you wouldn't *have* bad behaviour, you see, when you've been brought up respectable like we were. There's proper ways to behave, even if you've got nothing. *Mrs C*

Bad behaviour in other hoppers has only really occurred in recent years, according to Mrs D, and she believes that this happened only because of other changes that she has seen taking place in the world.

G: Did you ever have any trouble from the rough families?

Mrs D: No, not in them days. They was all people who went

to earn a shilling, weren't they, in them days? Well, though, when we was over at Brenchley, they had students there. They do that now, now there's machine picking. We was waiting for the hopping, so we was doing a bit of fruiting. And he had about eight there. But he had so much aggravation, you know, with them, that he had to get the police to take 'em off. They was smoking that stuff, and going silly, and doing soppy things. And so that's what they done: spoiled it.

The women said many things about the changes that they have witnessed, both 'down hopping' and in their lives in general. These are looked at in Chapter 11. But before hand picking finally came to an end, the women had the yearly experience of completing the harvest. They all had memories of the annual celebrations that marked the end of that year's picking and signalled that it was time to go back home to London.

10
Time to Go Home: The End of the Harvest

'It was the best night, a goodbye night.'

Everyone knew that whoever got to strip the last bine pulled would have good luck for the year to come. The atmosphere became celebratory as the harvest was almost completed for yet another year. The women would have their earnings to look forward to – if they hadn't already used them all up in subs, or by paying back the fare borrowed from the farmer to get there in the first place. The children might get treated to new ribbons or shoes for their return home, or at least an extra treat from the 'lolly man' who visited the hop farms with his tray of confectionery. The huts would have to be cleaned; hopping boxes re-packed; straw bedding burnt on huge bonfires; a coveted hop bine saved to tie to the front of the lorry for the journey home, and the return to their other lives in London. But before all this, there were the rituals and celebrations to observe.

Some of the traditions were obviously well established, as can be seen in Christopher Smart's poem, written in 1722. This is how he recorded the eighteenth century version of the harvest's end:

> The cumulating mob
> Strive for the mastery – who first may fill

The bellying bin, and cleanest cull the hops
Nor ought retards, unless invited out
By Sol's declining, and the evening's calm,
Leander leads Letitia to the scene
Of shade and fragrance – then th'exulting band
Of pickers, male and female, seize the fair
Reluctant, and with boisterous force and brute,
By cries unmov'd, they bury her i' th' bin;
Nor does the youth escape – him too they seize,
And in such posture place as best they serve
To hide his charmer's blushes; then with shouts
They rend the echoing air, and then from both –
So custom has ordained – a largess claimed.

Poetic language apart, the women recounted many similar stories of being thrown 'i' th' bin', just like the 'fair' young woman in the poem. They also talked of having their photographs taken with their arms draped with hop-laden bines or apple-laden branches; fertility rituals from a time earlier than even Christopher Smart's, changed to more manageable but still timeless symbols of fecundity, bringing 'good fortune' for the year to come.

All the special things we had to do. Yes. Like pulling the last bine, and throwing the girls in the bins. The pretty ones! I used to get worried, even when I was young. Worried that someone would get hurt. 'Cos instead of picking you up and laying you in like bin-wise, they'd just used to pick you up and toss you in. I was frightened someone would break their back. We'd all be a bit over-excited, sort of. Oh you used to be looking round the field see who was having the last bine. It was so good, I think we'd have done hopping for nothing, we used to enjoy all the things like that so much. Yes, we was all one. *Mrs AB*

I remember when it was my sister they threw in the bin. Right up in the air, she went. She was ever so pretty . . . It was good luck for the whole year, like who pulled the last bine. They'd all hang on to their bines to see if they could be the one to pull the last bine. Then when the last bine was finished they'd chuck all the girls in the bins! The men would've come down for the last day, and going home like. What a party there'd be! No one'd want to miss out on that. A good old knees up. *Mrs D*

But before the festivities could begin the huts would be tidied one final time. There was always the threat of rats and other infestations of 'wildlife', so it was important to leave the huts well cleaned for reasons of hygiene as well as pride. And anyway, the other hoppers would see whether you were 'doing the job right'.

Chuck your straw bedding on to the hopping fires, then you'd have one great big bonfire! Get you in the mood for the party! Clean the hut right out. Make it nice and clean. 'Cos you used to store some of your gear there till next year, see. Mind you, not all of them was allowed. Good thing and all, they'd have left 'em in a right old mess some of them. *Mrs AB*

Then as we was going, at the end, we used to pack all our things. As we was going. We'd burn all the beds. That was it. Ready for going home. Burn the beds. All the old straw and faggots. *Mrs D*

I still like a bonny [bonfire] you know? The feeling of burning all the old rubbish, getting rid of it all. Giving it a good poke with a stick. Just like down hopping! *Mrs S*

The clearing up finished for another year, the women would go and queue for their money. The farmers would sit behind a trestle table on the common, outside the huts, or in the yard. On the table would be the cash box and ledgers ready to check against the hoppers' books. If the records agreed, and the farmer agreed that no 'fiddling' had gone on, the pickers would collect their earnings. The amount varied according to what the harvest, and the weather, had been like. As mentioned earlier, any subs were deducted, and the farmer was then paid back any borrowed train fares.

That was the great day. We'd get paid out! Great day wasn't it? You'd go into the town that day. Mum'd buy us all new shoes and socks, and ribbons for our hair, to go home with, so that we'd all look nice. Respectable for the journey, and for people to see. That's how it used to be. Of course, if you picked up 60 quid between you's, like we did, we was fast pickers, see, you was millionaires then! Them days wasn't you? When you think what you could do with 60 quid. Yeh, well, I'll tell you, I used to come home, pay up me bit of rent what I owed, and one thing and another and still have a few bob saved for Christmas. No wonder it was a great day! All that money. And you could do so much with it then. Not like now! *Mrs D*

Money collected, packing done, the parties could begin. These varied according to the hoppers' taste and whether the farmer had decided to organise the activities. These 'organised' activities were often another means of controlling the hoppers. Having a meal and sports laid on at the farm meant that the Londoners would be kept out of the village and its pubs. The largest farms had yearly hop festivals at the end of picking, including barbecues, sports, even beauty contests to pick the hop princess. The smaller farms might have similar events, but often the pickers would, as they said, 'make their own entertainment', using a bit of their hard-earned money to pay for some food and drinks to share between them. Some of the families would do exactly as the farmers had anticipated and go into the village and blow most of their earnings in the pub. Others would get together to spend the last night round the fire, or have impromptu parties in the oast houses. If they didn't have enough money to buy extra supplies they simply used up any food and drink they had left – it saved having 'to take the grub home' anyway:

What I remember most was the last night. That was the night that everybody danced. And like a big ring-a-roses round the fire! Everything was cooked so we didn't have to take the grub home. And I think even the kids had a drop of stout. You know, in the old screw-top bottles. Like kind of stone they were the screw tops. The kids used to get a drop because the billy can wasn't full of tea *that* night! [Laughter] I think that was the *only* time the billy didn't see no tea. [Pause] The last night. [Pause] We'd really stay up late. Enjoying ourselves. Singing and dancing. You'd see the odd couple creep off down the fields and you'd say [silent gesture]. It was the best night, a goodbye night, you know. And it'd be all, 'See you next year!' And we'd shout out, laughing we'd be, 'Pull no more bines! See you! See you next year!' *Mrs AA*

The hoppers were on their way home for another year. Dressed in their weekend best for their triumphant return to London. Their old clothes, torn by the bines and stained black by the resin, were no longer needed. They had the whole year to collect more gear for the next harvest. Some locals claimed that the Londoners had no interest in how they left the countryside, and that they would simply toss their discarded garments into the hedge as they walked away down the lanes. This belief confirmed the locals' prejudices about the shameful ways of the 'dirty foreigners'.

They left the place in such a state that people would pray for rain to wash away the filth. The flood was like a final answer, washing away the muck for good. (Courier at the Whitbread Hop Museum)

Many of the women wouldn't have the chance ever to 'see you again next year'. For the pickers who worked on the farms whose owners had decided to change to mechanised harvesting, hopping was over for ever. They had made their last journey home.

11
Changes: It Was Different Then

'They was lovely times. They shouldn't be forgotten.'

They were magical times for me, and I will never forget them. I took my gran back to R [the farm where they had always picked] a couple of years before she died and I could still smell that wonderful smell of fruit, hops and flowers and all the marvellous, magical memories of big coloured dragonflies in the swamp by the Buttercup Meadow, the beautiful butterflies. The gypsy camp with their lovely coloured wagons. I wish I could have those days back. We never had much money or material things so we enjoyed nature to the full. There is nothing to take [hopping's] place. (Extract from a letter sent to me)

When the women talked about their memories of hopping, they seemed to have a shared understanding of what the past was like and what it had meant to them. They also had shared ideas about 'what has gone wrong' – the changes that have taken place to 'spoil' hopping, as Mrs D put it. They also had views on the reasons for the changes. Partly, it was seen as the fault of the machinery which had been introduced on to the farms, but the women sensed other problems. They talked about wider and deeper changes that had taken place. Life itself had changed for all of them. The change-over to machinery was a part of other, less objective, shifts which had altered and spoilt their lives.

G: Did you ever go when there were machines, A?

Mrs AA: No. I think a lot stopped going then. It was too commercialised. Now it's all changed. It's changed – the way of life – see?

The women I spoke to who had tried working with the mechanised system of harvesting did not think very highly of the new methods. Their traditional skills and experience were no longer needed for carrying out the factory-type job that hop picking had become. With the widespread use of machines, the picker's job had been reduced to standing in huge sheds 'cleaning' the hops. This involved picking over the machine-gathered cones to remove any leaves or debris from a relentlessly moving conveyor belt.

The employers still use mainly female labour – it is still 'suitable' work for women. It has been argued that this type of seasonal work is appropriate for women because of their 'natural' deftness with their 'nimble' fingers; an argument long used throughout the world to devalue and ghettoise traditional female occupations. From the (literally) blinding work of fine sewing and lace making to the more rugged jobs found in the box assembly industry, cheap female labour has been used on the pretext that it is suitable work to provide 'pin money' for nimble-fingered women. According to some farmers I spoke to, hopping is now also seen as suitable vacation work for students, both male and female, presumably until they get 'proper jobs'. As Farmer D had told me, it was only ever in times of economic depression and high unemployment that men picked; although old men, sick men and older boys would sometimes be employed. As soon as the men could get themselves 'real', more appropriate, jobs, then hop picking was seen as women's work once more. Farmer D never had the opportunity to employ students, as he did not have the acreage to justify investing in expensive machinery. But 'his' hand pickers remained loyal until he could no longer afford to grow hops. The farmers who have introduced mechanisation cannot depend on keeping their regular workers, and usually have to find new employees for the harvest.

We stopped and did a bit of hopping for him when he got a machine. But we didn't like that. It was standing picking the leaves out. I never went no more. I didn't like that. I give it up then and never went no more. I went once on the machine. 'Awww,' I said, 'I couldn't go on the machine no more.' Didn't like it. I only tried it for him [the farmer] because we'd been going there so long. And he said, 'You'll *love* it. It's so *easy*.' Oh gawd! The days dragged. No one talking to anybody else, 'cos you couldn't hear no one, 'cos of the machine, could you? The noise was terrific. Like a rotten factory. Used to pray for it to break down so's you could sit and pick a few by hand. Yeh. [Pause] We used to pick when it broke down. We prayed for it to break down. Just used to stand and pick the leaves out. They don't dry with the leaves in, see? Hops. *Mrs D*

Those who could bear to work in the sheds with the machinery were considered by the women who spoke to me as people with different values to the old hand pickers, people whose primary concern was the cash nexus . . .

They had a machine round there when I was working there. We went and saw it one day. But I wasn't much gone on it. Like being in a factory. The noise! You couldn't chat or nothing. It was the open air and all that sort of thing that people liked. It done *me* all right, mate! But now. They've got to grab the last shilling. You know what I mean? We never used to worry about that. They don't stop for lunch or nothing now. *No.* Just like factory piece work now. *Mrs AB*

My mother said that 'not stopping for lunch' probably meant

that the new breed of indoor hoppers don't take the nine o'clock break for something to eat and drink. Traditionally this was timed to follow the first measuring, about two hours into the hand pickers' day. The old pickers called that break 'lunch' as their mid-day meal was usually referred to as their 'dinner'.

Like the introduction of the factory methods of production at the time of the industrial revolution, the pickers who decided to work with the machinery were tied to a different system of time-keeping and working, the mechanical 'tyranny' of the clock replacing the traditional breaks governed by daylight and hunger. Complaints similar to those documented as being voiced during the early years of industrial production abound in the hoppers' views on mechanised harvesting. The women equated factory work with the misery of silent, alienated labour, the very conditions they had to endure during the rest of their working year.

Think. They're on machines. And they only have a fortnight now. Not like when we'd all be down there, all laughing and chatting round the bins. Having a lark. What's the point? Might as well stay at home for that. *Mrs RR*

It *was* a break from the routine. Now that's all it is – another bloody routine! *Mrs S*

The passing of the old ways were deeply regretted by all the women. Like many ex-pickers, Mrs M's time down hopping had given her the ambition to move to Kent, which she had done on her husband's retirement. She had always thought that living close to the hop gardens she would be able to go hopping again, but the introduction of machinery had made her reconsider. She didn't know whether she would be able to pick, whether the changes would be too upsetting for her to bear.

Oh we enjoyed it so much. Only the other day we were still saying, 'Let's go hopping. We wouldn't even have to stop there!' But those machines though. I don't think we could. It

would be a real disappointment I think. I wouldn't like that.
It would spoil everything. *Mrs M*

It isn't just the pickers who resent the changes. Other farmers
share Mr D's regrets that their budgets mean that they are being
left behind in the spread of mechanisation. Both of the following comments are from ex-hop farmers.

Wouldn't pay to continue with hops, what they want for a
machine today. That's only for the big boys.

Lot of the land is being turned over to so-called 'leisure'.
There seems to be money around for that.

As the owners of small farms are forced by commercial
pressure to give up hop growing, hop cultivation and the labour
to service it become increasingly geared towards the impersonal
relationships of industrial employer and employee.

The old times have all gone. These machine pickers. Just do
it for the money. But really there wouldn't be another reason
to go hopping. Not now. It's not like it was, you see. The
money's the only thing it's got . . . Mind you, money's the
only thing most of them think about today. If you was going
for anything like *we* used to go for, you wouldn't get it. Not
today. *Mrs J*

Money was cited as being responsible for many of the other
changes so disliked by the women. They described people today
as being 'selfish', 'greedy' and in constant 'competition' with
others. Values (and needs) were seen to have changed, mostly
for the worse. Mrs L was a bit more optimistic, however; she
thought that people hadn't changed completely for the worse.

People have different expectations now. People used to say,
'Right, hop picking, that's my level. I won't go anywhere
else.' Kids now know there's something different. And more.

Our standards of living have changed, and the children are used to *that* standard. They say, 'I'm not going round their house, it's a tip.' They notice other levels. Or, 'They've got a smashing place,' they say. It does rule some people's lives, but we should want better things and opportunities. *Mrs L*

Mrs L's was really a lone, and younger, voice among those who regretted the passing of the old ways and the coming of new, more materialistic values.

. . . I don't think people can talk now. Not like they used to. Everybody's got a bit more snobbish, I think. Nobody had anything then so there was nothing to be snobbish about. But now Londoners have bettered themselves – great big houses in Virginia Water. Surrey! They look down their noses at us now. See I still regard myself as a Londoner, even though I live out in the country now. Maybe in a few years' time they'll say, 'Oh! Are you really from London? You don't sound it.' But to me, I'll always come from London. London's home, sort of thing. Even though I was dragged up. I started at the *bottom*. I've changed in some ways. I used to swear like a trooper, but not so bad now. I have changed, but I still think of myself as a Londoner. *Mrs AA*

When you think about how our standards have changed . . . If mine don't have a bath every bleeding day they think it's World War Three broke out. You should have heard 'em when the immersion heater broke down! *Mrs RR*

Like Mrs M, Mrs AB moved from London to the Kent countryside, fulfilling the dream shared by so many people who had been hop picking. But the move hasn't protected her from the changes that she feels have spoilt her life.

I'll tell you what the trouble is now – one's frightened the other one's got a shilling more than the other one. Now that's a lot of the problem. That is, honestly. They can't all be on a

level. It's disgusting how they go on. See if you've got nothing, years ago, if you got nothing it made no difference. You was all one. But *now*. Not now. 'I'm getting on better than her and that's it.' It's not right. That's all they want to know or care about. [Posh voice] 'Oh I've seen *that* before, on that woman that she "does for" up there.' 'Oh look at that coat, you know where she got that.' It is. It's disgusting.
Mrs AB

Most of the women are certainly living in more comfortable physical conditions than they had in the past. Their financial circumstances have also, generally, improved. This might be due to the fact that they no longer have young families to support but, except for Mrs L, their feeling is that their quality of life is worse.

When people got more money in their pockets it was Spain and all that. I don't know sometimes. I think [pause] the old days were better. No aggravation. No jealousy. No 'She's got this, got that.' Our sister! Well she has to keep getting new stuff *all* the time . . . This is our original three-piece suite. Now it's who's got the best dress on tonight when you have holidays. True? *Mrs M*

Their kids have everything. That's it. Every *thing*. Pity they don't have love. They think they give them things and it's all right. It's not. People have got no time for one another. *Mrs S*

Times have changed so much. There's Rollers down on our old farm. Going down hopping! And it's not unusual to see Bentleys and Mercedes down there. All showing what they've got. They go to the community place, the club, but you don't get the singsongs like you used to. Too good for that now, I suppose. Even though they was hard times, you can't say that it's changed for the better. *Mrs J*

Mrs B explained how she also saw cars as representing part of the undesirable changes that have taken place. As a village shopkeeper the expansion in the ownership of private cars has made a major, unwelcome, impact on her whole way of life, the old, shared life of a community reduced to individual, privatised existences.

In the end we named it the 'Forget Me' shop. They'd all got cars. The locals too. *So* they'd buy their bits here that they'd forgot after they'd been to Tunbridge Wells for their main shopping. If we were lucky. Sort of made a convenience out of us. After all them years of serving them all . . . But oh it did upset me so much when my husband decided to close it. It really did. I missed it. I missed all the people. They'd go to those great big shops. They don't even know who you are. You don't even have to talk to anyone. They wouldn't ask how your children are, would they? *Mrs B*

Mrs C described how, ironically, even the improvements in her life heralded unwanted changes.

Course, when we got posh we brought a toilet seat down. [Laughing] To have our own toilet top. Well now they even have their own toilets! Imagine that. A shed behind your hut with a chemical lav. You keep your own toilet locked, just for you, see? *Well.* That's not hopping. Hopping is *not* hopping! They're trying to make it posh. I've always said this for years and years. Hop picking's a glorified – no reverse that – a caravan holiday is a glorified hop picking holiday, *without* the fun. That's why they go in caravans, to pretend it was like down hopping. Well, it's *not.* The life, definitely the life, made it fun. People have changed it. People have got so selfish and greedy. 'Cos everyone's trying to keep up with the Joneses. I wish we could go back to how it was. The holiday. The people. Lovely. [Pause] People have all changed through trying to keep up with the Joneses. It's like everything else. They get greedy. I've got more now, but it don't make you happy. It was better then, wasn't it? *Mrs C*

Spending holidays abroad had become a possibility for many of the people I spoke to during the research. But Mrs R considers these locations inferior to going hopping. Foreign holidays, she felt, meant going without the sort of company that she cared for, but included the competitive aspects she despised.

I think that if it came back and like R went, I went, and A went, and like the people we know, it would be ideal. It would be a real lark. Like I'm going away in a few weeks to Corfu. It's all, 'Have you got the right frock on?', for going down to dinner and all that. I can't be bothered with all that. You know. I mean down there it was all just mucking in. It was entirely different. You didn't *have* anything to take, did you? It was great. We'd all take all the old gear down there and share what we did have. No competitions. Even though it was that bleeding hut. All the kids. It was a lark! We was all happy! *Mrs R*

Mrs D also reminisced about being happy. She described a scene: a group of happy people sitting outside a hopping hut around a huge table that was covered with food and drinks. They were having an impromptu party – the sort of occasion that contributed to the 'holiday' that many of the women would love to have again.

That was a party! There was some travellers staying. Nice sort of people. And we wound up having this lovely party. We all went to it. It was one of the little children's birthdays, and they'd never had a birthday party. So we all done all the trimmings. All of us. For them. And we done this lovely party. And it turned into a beer party later! [Laughing] We was up all night, but it was good. Yeh, we used to do things like that for one another. That's what made it. Different to holidays now. All keeping themselves to themselves. All posh clothes. We tried holiday camp once, me and my husband. *Once*. Ain't never been since. My daughter was looking at some photos when I got them out, 'Weren't they good days, Mum? Better than Spain.' Like she goes to Spain now. She said, 'Oh I wish I could go again.' Young kids have got *no* idea. It's all artificial, innit? You know, it was a lovely life. People don't realise. *Mrs D*

I visited the women who agreed to do taped interviews on several occasions. After the initial meetings with the women, several said that it was the first evening in a long time that they could remember sitting talking to someone. Usually they would turn on their television sets until bedtime. The isolation of their present lives was seen in definite and negative contrast to the community living that hopping had come to represent in their memories.

People are more selfish and greedy. And I think more begrudging. See you can't say they quarrel more, it's not that. It's not. It's 'What have you got?' Like a competition. Yes, I think it is. Everything's altered. It's all different. Telly altered your *total* way of living, didn't it? Getting up at seven o'clock to watch telly. It seems unnatural when you think of it. All just sitting there watching telly. *Mrs C*

The isolation was experienced and described in a variety of ways. Mrs AB felt this about it:

They come along now to wait for a bus and sometimes they hardly say, 'Hello'. No they don't. Not even that. The telly, all in their own front rooms. Yes, we was all one then. You'd help one another. But now. You just get taken for granted. Well, you go in a pub now, you see. They're all in little groups here and little groups there. You used to go in and everyone'd say, 'Hello! Hello!' even if they didn't know you. Now you sit there all night and no one says a bleeding word to you. *Mrs AB*

According to Mrs C and Mrs S even the weather has taken a turn for the worse. The old days really were the golden days in their memories.

Mrs C: Lovely summers. Lovely summers.

Mrs S: Why did we always have beautiful summers for that six weeks?

Mrs C: I don't know. But even as children you had wonderful summers. You never had summers like this.

Mrs S: We were saying the other day, 'Why was hop picking weather always so beautiful?' I don't know.

These women, members of my family and other people I spoke to, were all certain that they had remembered the weather correctly. It had been wonderful. It is, of course, often noted that the weather of our past, particularly of our child-hood, seems better than the present climate, but so many people were so convinced that I tried to check their stories. I contacted the Bracknell Meteorological Station enquiries department and spoke to a meteorologist who also turned out to be an amateur psychologist. He assured me that:

No, the climate does not change so drastically. Any changes between 1920 and 1970, for instance, would have been very subtle. But it is a feature of human nature to remember good days and forget the bad. One's memory is always of the happy days.

The meteorologist offered to chart rainfall patterns in Kent for that period, but the cost (and, really, a desire not to know) precluded me from accepting his invitation. Again he reassured me that any changes would have been 'very subtle'. His assurances were given to me before 'green awareness' had brought the destruction of the ozone layer to the layperson's attention. Perhaps the representative from Bracknell might not be so convinced of his 'facts' today.

The passage of time *might* have distorted our memories about the subtleties of change in weather patterns, but the women are certain of one thing: for them it is a fact that the past was a safer place in which to live. The isolation felt by them in their current lives – whether due to people sitting in their 'own front rooms watching telly', or because of the dispersal of the old London communities in which they once made their homes – caused the sense of fear and anxiety which they all talked about. That is the change they disliked most.

You could leave your places then, see? You couldn't now. It's all bolts and bars now. I put my chain on as soon as it gets dark. If it's five o'clock I put the chain on. Not like it was. It used to be lovely. *Mrs AB*

My son says to me when he goes, 'You will lock up, Mum, won't you?' And they made me get a phone extension in the bedroom, in case of intruders. *Mrs B*

I've got an Alsatian. You can't be too careful. *Mrs S*

Mrs D believes that it is increasing affluence which has led to the breed of criminal who violated her beautiful home. It seems tragic that someone who takes such pride and care in the decoration of her house should be the victim of this type of attack:

Never had no thieves then. If they'd got in they'd have given *me* something. We never had nothing. What did you have? I'll tell you. Nothing. We never even had a key, to tell you the truth, love. Nothing. We lived down our street all our lives. Our mother had all of us there. In the same house. And never had a key all our life there. Never had a key for the door. [Pause] Just put the key through the door on a string if people did want 'em. *Now*! Cor, bolt and bar up, don't you? Well you're frightened to go out really, ain't you? Well, went out one day, quarter to eleven and come back half past twelve. They'd been here. Tore me place to bits. I'll never forget it. I can even tell you the exact date. It nearly killed me. And me bed. Well I don't know what they expected to find in it. They tore it literally to pieces. They even opened up the pillows. I went straight upstairs. I should never have done that. The policeman said, 'They could have killed you.' But, you know, that's how it's got, hasn't it? It's terrible. *Mrs D*

Mrs RR spoke about the contrast between how people live today, in their interior, lonely existences and how people were more visible in the neighbourhoods of the 'old days'. She said that everyone was more aware of what was happening in their street, and in their immediate locality, because life was centred out of doors. It was a parochial existence, but it was communal. Perhaps memories about the fine weather were more accurate than the meteorologist would accept; the street culture of the past was described as being almost Mediterranean in its warmth and liveliness. I certainly remember much of my childhood being centred on the street. Not at all the sort of behaviour to be inspired by grey skies and rain.

They was different times then. Different times. It was always safer then. Or so they all said! But it was lovely then. I can't remember any arguments. We all spoke to one another. We was all friends. All the mucking in together. But that wasn't just hopping, was it? It's how it used to be down your street, didn't it? Everyone knew each other. It was. [Pause] You always had your door open in the summer. Everyone was sitting outside. We'd take chairs out and sit out there gassing till right late. The kids was all playing. You lived on the street. *Mrs RR*

All the kids'd be sitting on the kerbs, and the old girls'd be on their old kitchen chairs they'd fetched out or on the steps. Sometimes you'd get the 'Jazzers' come round. They'd sing songs and we'd all join in. Throw 'em a few coppers. All the kids'd chase after them up the road. See where they was going next. Your mums wouldn't be worried. They'd know you was all all right. *Mrs S*

Mrs M and her husband recalled similar London street scenes from their courting days.

Mr M: Hopping was like back in London. You actually lived out in the streets. Lovely night like this, when I was courting Mrs M, there'd be all different people at their doors: 'Goodnight F! Goodnight T!'

Mrs M: Too hot to shut your doors. You'd just sit there. We weren't afraid. We'd just sit there as long as we wanted. Never had any locks on the door. Never had anything! If we wanted anything we'd have to save for it. Mind a baby for a penny when we was kids. The war changed everything. The 1914 war changed things. The 1939 war changed things. People have changed. They're all watching the same things on the telly on their individual sets. Even in the same family! They have more than one telly you see. We've lost the community. You don't think any more in the evenings, right, 'Out come the cards.' Used to listen to the wireless. All together we'd sit. Then we did all used to sit round. And then, play cards, or up me sister's we'd go. We'd all play. Play cards with her and her husband. All of us. Mr M's sister used to come round, and her husband as well. We used to just play. No money attached at all. [Pause] And now we say, 'The bad old days!' I don't think so.

Mr M: The difference is, now there's fear in everybody. That's the thing. Years ago, you didn't have fear. I've been today and put two bolts on the lady up the road's door. Two or three people I've done that for. Years ago you never had it. It's fear that does it. 'Why should I work? I'll break in here.' That's what the attitude is now. We never had it.

Mrs M: And that was another thing. We all kept together.

How 'true' the women's, and my, memories of 'life in the streets in the old days' might, or might not, be does not matter. Perhaps the meteorologist's amateur psychoanalysis, that we were only remembering the 'happy' bits of our past lives, was accurate. What does matter is that the women *remember* the past as being safer, as being different. Their explanations for the differences, however, were *not* always shared. Two of the women I spoke to gave a specific reason for their fear and the changes they perceived in their lives. The following quote is fairly representative of their views:

The reason for leaving London was the wogs taking over all the houses and jobs. My nan has to have bolts and bars on her doors now. It's not safe any more. We used to be out playing till half past ten. Eleven, when it was light. My nan knew that I'd go out and come back the same as when I went out. But I think Londoners will always be Londoners. It's just the environment that's changed. Bloody high-rise blocks. They've pulled so much of London down. And wogs. I mean that's something you never saw down hopping, a wog. Londoners are still Londoners but it will never be the same as it was. The women at work say I was born too late, that I should have been alive in the thirties. 'Cos that to me was when you was able to leave your front door open then. Before they all come here.

It is an understatement to say that I felt surprised and discomfited when racist comments were made by the women during the interviews. These comments (usually) were made in the context of our discussions about change and loss of community. The women with whom I was speaking were often distressed about the changes they were describing. The people they were blaming were being used as a target, a focus for their anger. Ironic really when they themselves had been dismissed and vilified by others as being 'foreigners'. My reactions to the women's racism can only be described as a feeble, half-hearted challenge. I admit that I did not know how to deal with those situations. Without attempting to justify my behaviour, I want to express why I felt genuinely ambivalent: I was a stranger invited into their houses; I had come to value the relationships with the women which had developed during the year I was meeting with them. But I was also confronted with this open hostility against black and Asian people – the people whose very existence was being presented to me as a major facet of some of the women's understanding of the changes which had spoilt their lives. The conflict was between being angered myself and showing it in being judgmental of their views (slipping into a white, academically-informed anti-racist speech) and accepting the women's versions of their lives. My actual spoken reaction to these statements was along the lines of expressing my disagreement with any arguments that put unsupported blame on any group of people. I suggested that it was necessary to look at underlying reasons and explanations for the changes. I made an ineffective grasp at the Political, the Social and the Cultural . . . I tried to retain a critical view of the past without being hostile to the women. They were, after all, the subjects, not the objects, of this book.

But whatever the reasons the women found for the changes in their lives, and however they had come to perceive them, they all regretted the passing of a time that had meant so much to them.

Hop picking had meant so many different things: a source of extra cash; a holiday in the beautiful Kent countryside; a reunion with old friends; another 'hopping baby'; communal living; escape from a violent husband; 'a right lark'; a break from urban squalor; 'horrible loos'; the chance of getting somebody's hand-me-downs; 'sharing looking after the kids'; being helped when you needed it; and a chance to help others when they needed you.

For the women I spoke to, 'things are not like they were' any more, and they are saddened by their loss. The time when 'we was all one' has passed and, for them at least, no more bines are being pulled.

These then are the memories of the past, and the views on why things have changed, of some London women who went hop picking.

It was like a foreign land, wasn't it? *Mrs T*

Part 2

12
On Reflection: Oral History

At the end of a work like this there is usually a conclusion making observations about, and comments on, the 'material' included in the book. In this case, that material is made up of the memories and stories which the women contributed in the form of their oral testimony. On reflection I feel that it would be an impertinence for me to 'conclude' on their lives. I have instead decided to discuss some of the issues surrounding the nature and use of oral testimony as evidence. Issues concerning evidence are relevant to many types of writing but I believe there is a need to address these more thoroughly and openly in the presentation of oral history. It might sound like blasphemy to some, but my experience has shown that the creation of an oral history is not a democratic process . . .

Oral History: Use or Abuse?

I had two main reasons for wanting to produce an oral history about women from East London who had been hop picking: first, I had shared that experience and remembered it with pleasure; second, from my reading on the subject I had understood oral history to be an egalitarian practice in which working class women could write themselves into history through, and by, their own words.

> Oral history can be a tool for re-writing history from the bottom up, through the words of the people who experienced it.[1]

> Oral history gives history back to the people in their own words. And in giving a past, it also helps them towards a future of their own making.[2]

So, both my personal history and my political interest in equality made me feel a particular engagement with both the form and the content of such a book. I began the work loaded with assumptions about how an oral history project would develop. But during the course of the year and a half in which I researched the history I became aware of the limitations and the problematic nature of working with oral history.

An unequal power relationship between the historian (me) and the informants (the women who told me their stories) became increasingly apparent as I selected and organised the themes and the chapters, the words and the supporting evidence. This editorial power was very different from what I might have expected from reading some recent women's history which presents an almost unquestioning privileging of the 'truth' of women's lived experience.

But I still think that oral history has a radical potential. It can provide the empirical data on which to base theoretical analysis. Oral history can provide information about the cultural processes which lead us to develop specific versions of ourselves through our memories; it can look at not only what those meanings represent, but also at how they can further our oppressions by reinforcing the engendered social relations in which we live.

Oral history also has a very practical value: it is a repository of our past. This came to have a very personal significance for me. After doing the initial research, which took me about 18 months, my house was flooded with sewage. The result was that we, my family, lost everything on the ground floor of our home. This included most of our photographs. The ones from my children's early years were a particular loss for us all. The first draft of this book was also destroyed. At first I was so upset by the flood, and stressed by the disruption to our lives, that the book was the furthest thing from my mind. Gradually I came to realise that I had to start again. I thought about the stories my grandmother had told me, and about how we can forget. I wanted to make every effort to create a permanent record. I had learned another lesson about valuing memories.

Method

To begin the work I started speaking to women from the East End of London, including members of my family, who had been hop picking in Kent. We discussed our experiences and memories. Initially, the people I met were already known to me, but soon word got round about what I was doing, and I found that many other women wanted to talk about going hopping. I contacted other informants by various means. Some of the contacts were made through immensely satisfying 'detective' work – a real pleasure when compared with other parts of the research which involved looking through dust-covered newspapers in lonely libraries.

I also spoke with farmers, brewery representatives, ex-shopkeepers, men and women who run pubs and, via the telephone, with various anonymous voices from the National Farmers' Union, English Hops Ltd and Wye College, Kent.

Ten women agreed to my taping a series of extended interviews, as well as taking handwritten notes during our briefer discussions. This involved *them* in allowing me to make several visits to their homes, and involved *me* in having many hours of recorded material to transcribe for each visit I made. Transcribing the tapes was a long and difficult process, particularly as I do not have typing skills. (I have a secret wish that I hadn't resisted learning to use a keyboard!) I had to keep stopping the tape recorder to replay sections in order to make sure that the transcription was accurate. There was the additional problem of trying to interpret the tapes when so many of the words were hidden by us laughing.

These difficulties all had their associated frustrations, but a genuine dilemma presented itself when I had to decide how to transcribe the spoken words to account for accent, pronunciation and rhythm. My first attempts left me with what looked like a script for a jolly cockney sit com, of the 'Cor blimey! Strike a light, mate' variety. My own London accent, for instance, always sounds awful to me on recordings, but on paper everyone's words looked ridiculous. My solution was to include phonetic renderings of speech if these seemed relevant to the accurate conveyance of meaning.

Other problems which arose from the selection and organisation of the material, and the positioning of myself in the text, are discussed below, but I want to say here that the material was never selected because it gave the most lively read: the material simply *is* fascinating.

During the discussions I always had a basic structure of questions to use as a general guide. This was particularly useful in the taped sessions. It served as a reminder of the topics I wanted to find out about, and was something to shuffle and look at during the silences and lulls in our conversations. It took me a while to learn that these silences were important, and that I shouldn't act like a hostess at a dinner party by filling any gaps with trite chatter.

The following general areas cover the list of topics that I wanted to discuss during the interviews:

- basic biographical details

- family and friends

- domestic and paid work

- pleasure and leisure

- relationships with other pickers and the locals

- why people went picking

- community and privacy
- changes in the women's lives

When a particular issue, such as waiting to get the hopping letter, was referred to on a number of tapes I made a point of asking the other women about it in our future meetings.

I hope that the methods I used to collect the testimonies have done justice to the lives of the women who were kind enough to trust me with their time and their memories. The pleasures of having the discussions certainly seemed mutual. We laughed a lot. One of the recordings, when Mrs RR and Mrs T were together, was punctuated by more fits of laughter than usual. It was impossible to listen to the tape without seeing Mrs T recounting her amazing war-time adventures with a balloon and a grumpy WRAC officer. That incident wasn't 'relevant' to this particular text – a reminder that there are many histories left unwritten, and also that history can be fun.

During the taping sessions women were moved to tears as well as laughter. Mrs B began to sob when she recalled the days when hop pickers had been customers in her shop. I asked her if she would like me to stop for a while. 'Oh no!' she said, 'I'm really enjoying it!' She found pleasure in her memories. And so did I.

I can do no better in summarising this section than to quote from Marilyn Porter's summary of the process of working with oral testimony:

As everyone with tape-recorded material knows, transcription and analysis are long and tedious. At times there is a danger of becoming too distant from the field experience. Faces fade and are replaced by colour-coded cards. Still analysis must happen. I reorganised my material, imposed categories; I began to write, I was aware of gaps in my material it was too late to fill. I was also aware that the fieldwork had a beginning and an end. I talked to all the people at a specific historical moment, both in their own lives and in public history of this country . . . In the end I have written a tribute to the people who talked to me. I could not let them remain silent because of my failure to write. And indeed, if the [people] . . . in this study can speak to us they shquld give us confidence in the undying vitality of [the] working class . . .[3]

Critical Reflections on the Use of Oral Testimony

History is like a series of photograph albums, typically showing us 'important people' at 'important moments' that have taken a particular photographer's fancy. Oral history is more like the great march of time frozen in a family snapshot. It's nothing new to say that *all* history, whatever its topic, is subjective – in this respect, this work is no different – but I do want to make a particular point about this book: that I am, in a number of ways, more overtly part of the subject of this history than might usually be the case. I share many experiences with the women around whose testimonies this book is centred: I was taken hop picking as a girl; I came from a similar class and geographical location; my spoken language is similar. I have also entered the writing openly and acknowledge both a personal and an ideological investment in doing so. These points are obviously important to the way in which the history was eventually produced.

Although the components that make up this history are 'real', the shapes I have made with them are, by the nature of the rules of ideology, *fictionalised*. The original experiences recounted by the women (picking, laughing, poverty, sharing) are objective events in that they happened in a reality, in their lived experience, but the history is an artifice, a creative reforming and restating of events no matter how sympathetic or empathic the historian. Like our contemporary video-recorded, filmic view of the world, this history is as edited and contrived as a mediaeval chronicle. It is doubly illusory if this representation is not recognised as a subjective interpretation. In support of this action of restating, however, I think that it is possible to express other people's ideas and experiences in ways which can enhance them, making them accessible and alive to readers. The women have found an arena in which to have their memories heard and acknowledged. This is not an attempt to make grandiose claims for this book, but to explain the purpose of collecting the oral testimonies and the remaking of them into this history.

Within the context of representing the intention behind the spoken words of others, it is necessary to recognise that without rigorous efforts to ensure the validity of interpretations, a would-be interpreter can drift very far of the mark. Sometimes everything can be lost in the translation. I saw a television programme about an anthropologist's attempt to present an honest version of the everyday lives of a group of tribal people. She had lived with the subjects of her study for some time, filming their lives and recording their conversations. She had decided to use sub-titles which translated their own speech, rather than the more conventional technique of having an omniscient narrator reciting a mediating script. One distinctive sequence stands out in my memory – the filming of an annual ritual. The camera operators were busy recording all the exotic details (*perfect for television*); they then moved in for a close-up shot of two women leaving a hut. The women were carrying an object. The camera moved in closer, eager for the most intimate shot of the treasure in their hands. It was a golden honeycomb. The two women paused and looked at each other. They spoke. The subtitle told us that one of them said: 'Why are they filming our lunch?'

Each version of a story has its own truth. And our myths, whether of the universal, numinous kind or of the more prosaic, family variety, are used by us to tell and retell truths in ways that mean we can make sense of our world. Of course there will be contradictions arising from competition between myths: my truth is often your tall story. How is it decided which of the alternative versions will win? Is it the one with the loudest voice which then lifts itself from the confines of myth into the powerful realms of being the new orthodoxy – the Truth? Is it at that point that the subject becomes object, subjectivity becomes objectivity? I suppose that it really depends on who gets the last laugh rather than the last word.

Who has the last word?

And so, in my role as editor, I have been present throughout the text. Even though I reject the notion of authorial omniscience (you have been adding your own significance to the material throughout your reading), it is I *who have made* the oral history from the 'raw material'. I did this through the processes of selection, organisation, juxtaposition and silencing the various constituents of the evidence. The interpretative framing, therefore, is mine.

In practical terms, this framing was done, initially, at a distance, a step back from the words. An underlying assumption as I worked on the material was that I had made relationships with the living women, not with the tape recordings and notebooks. Once the words became separated from their speakers, once I had transcribed the tapes on to paper, they took on an additional significance. The words no longer had simple, transparent meanings, they had become items of evidence. My efforts to present the stories honestly, however, were tempered by my concern to represent the women in a dignified manner. I hope that my being respectful to the women involved has not weakened or distorted the meanings of their words.

One particular word caused me the most problems: the word 'history'. As I started to write, all the magical connotations were there: *history and telling the truth as it happened*. I began to worry. Were the women's, and my, memories true or were they just stories? I realised that I had no 'innocent' sources of evidence – facts. I had, instead, the stories and their tellers' reasons for remembering in their own particular ways. I was dealing with multiple versions of the 'Truth'. The burden of responsibility for dealing with the evidence, for having the last word, was growing.

It was something of a relief to read an article by Alessandro

Portelli from which the following extract is taken:

> The first thing that makes oral history different . . . is that it
> tells us less about events as such than about their meaning.
> This does not imply that oral history has no factual interest;
> interviews often reveal unknown events or unknown aspects
> of known events, and they always cast new light on unex-
> plored sides of the daily life of the non-hegemonic classes . . .
>
> But the unique and precious element which oral sources
> force upon the historian . . . is the speaker's subjectivity . . .
> They tell us not just what people did, but what they wanted to
> do, what they believed they were doing, what they now think
> they did.[4]

Women's History and Feminist History

A history that seeks to record the experiences of working class
women is as problematic as the 'History', beloved of the
traditionalists, which records dates and battles. The making
visible, in a textual form, of a previously ignored sphere of
women's experience, by a woman producer, does not automati-
cally bestow value on the final product. The process of creating
that product must be examined.

To 'do work on women' can be a simplistic, essentialist
categorisation of women as raw material by those in the
privileged position of carrying out such research. But women's
history is important. It can have an empowering and even (dare
we say it today?) a consciousness-raising function. Women's
history can complete the record and thus obviate the need for a
continual reinventing of the feminist wheel. It is pertinent to
quote Alice Clarke's point made at the beginning of her book,
The Working Life of Women in the Seventeenth Century,
published in 1919:

> Hitherto the historians have paid little attention to the
> circumstances of women's lives, for women have been re-
> garded as a static factor in social developments.

This was forgotten by most people for a long time – in fact for the span of time between Alice Clarke's writing it and the so-called second wave of feminism. If women's history is not recorded, women's places in the world can be relegated to the condition of 'natural' stasis; the challenge to received wisdom about gender and power can go unspoken, except amongst groups of informed women and 'aware' men. A self-conscious theorising of the uses of history is needed for its effective practice in the service of equality.

The question is, how can history be made politically useful in feminist terms? Women's history certainly need not be feminist in intent or result (nor in terms of the processes of its making and distribution), so in what ways should a feminist critique of the past–present relationship be developed?

History has been used frequently as a retaining support for the power structures of dominant groups – notably in attempts to wipe out unacceptable events through a rewriting of the past. Examples of this can be seen in pre-revolutionary Nicaragua, or more recently in post-Tiananmen China. It is therefore essential in terms of gaining political power to confront the normalising processes prevalent in the dominant forms of what is accepted as conventional, orthodox 'History'.

The acceptable, most widely distributed, versions of the past are those which serve the interests of the status quo, the 'hegemonic classes' in Portelli's terms. Even 'our' memories of the past are mediated through images of 'then', represented to us now, through advertisements, school textbooks, or in Foucault's term, through popular memory.

General questions about the politics of recounting the past have a particular relationship with a history *about* women:

1 When working class women are the 'material' being studied, can the problem of objectification be separated from the satisfaction (and pleasure) of being 'written into history'?

2 Who actually profits from the text? Not a question about money (not many people get rich from writing history), but a

question about who benefits from the process and the final product.

3 Who is the consumer of the women's lives as represented by the historian? In other words, who reads the historical text (reads, no matter in what form the text is finally produced) and in what ways is it read?

4 Where is it acknowledged in this (or that) text 'on' women that physical conditions of production are involved in the making of a text (book, exhibit, film, whatever), as are the women who have a part (or not) in that process?

These questions formed part of the framework on which this history was made.

I concluded that more usual, scholarly concerns about authentic representation of evidence are laudable (if they are rigorous), but that they can be a red herring when dealing with oral testimony. Like autobiography, history, and particularly oral history, is partial in both senses of the word. That, surely, is part of its aim. A more pressing need is for an acknowledgment of the *process* of historical production (or of almost any other endeavour that I can think of). In this way, a project can be feminist even if the work is not 'on' women.

A feminist critique, say, of architecture, would be concerned as much with *how* the discipline is taught, by whom, to whom, where, when, and for what purposes as much as with the more overt ideological implications of design and aesthetics, the intended use, funding, cost and accessibility of the finished product.

For as long as traditional history remains the dominant model women's history can remain an interesting side issue. More volumes on the subject 'Woman' might be published and the topic 'Women and . . .' might get more index space in other texts, but the paradigmatic role of 'History' survives unchallenged.

A corrective to the lack of representations of women in

orthodox historical work is needed, but so too is the interven-
tion of a critique of the meanings of those representations
wherever, and whenever, women are included for study.

The continuous attempts to establish such a challenge need a
more concerted campaign than currently exists if there is going
to be a genuine subversion and disruption of the status quo, its
received wisdom and disabling myths. By the rigorous examination of the ontological meanings given to 'woman' we can
refute the constructions by analyses of our own.

A retreat into impotent relativism is not the point of retelling
the women's stories. The resolution of conflicting arguments
between competing myths is not an elegant game of settling
disputes about 'what really happened', or 'what the past
meant'. The point, for me, is crystallised by asking what the
past *means*, in terms of the meaning it has for us now – the
contradictions and differences informing us as much the same-
ness of our lives.

Further Reflections on Oral History

I had decided that an examination of the relationship between
past and present did not depend on whether or not the women's
stories were true. But for me to make sense of, and to use, the
evidence in a meaningful way was another huge responsibility
to the women. I had to ask how 'typical' the women were, if
they were to be representative sources of evidence. I became
concerned with whether an individual's experience *could* be
representative of a period of time, a geographical location, a
whole group of people. The reality of the arbitrary nature of the
framework of history which I had constructed began to worry
me.

The question of typicality seemed less urgent when I wondered whether it would make any difference to a historian
whether she was acting as an interpreter of a Roman pot or of
an oral testimony. The act of interpretation always carries the
burden of selection and of claiming expertise, no matter how

embarrassing or discomfiting that thought might be. The historian has to accept the responsibilities: whether examining a pot or listening to a story, she still arrives at conclusions by looking at evidence; through her efforts to comprehend she imposes a pattern and creates relevance.

For this book, the women gave accounts of their lives, then the historian, with all her presuppositions and cultural baggage, looked for supporting evidence, used comparative knowledge from other sources, and tied the whole lot into a tidy package, ready to be unpacked by the discerning reader. Does this process mean that the rigorous historian can understand the experience of the women more clearly than they do themselves?

I don't think so.

I think that's the job of poets.

Acknowledging all these reservations, I have tried to be as conscientious as possible in presenting the evidence, including my own, fairly. Explorations into our history allow us to question and make sense of our world, to create a critique of other people's versions of our lives. The development of a critical awareness is a major step towards gaining real power. It should be possible to be critical of historical source material without being hostile to its subjects. I tried to achieve this, even though it was at times a very difficult process.

The most difficult moment for me was when I was faced with racist explanations of change. I am more able to respond in this written text than I was in the women's homes – an undeniable acknowledgment of authorial responsibility and the absence of equality in such writing; another aspect of the complex relationship between the oral historian and the object and subjects of her work.

Spoken and written words
The partnership which exists between the oral historian and her living sources is not based on equality. This cannot be left without further consideration of the spoken and written words. I had the power to have the last word: to comment on and to question the women's words once they were typed on to the

page. This is in telling contrast to my comparative lack of power when sitting in someone's armchair, drinking her tea, taking her time. My presence in the text, whether overt or less obvious, meant that I could take cover behind the (literal) authority that I had. To have placed the women's words on the page without any comment would have meant that I had made something other than this book. I made this book in the way that I chose, deciding which of the taped words were, or were not, included. I reiterate, the practice of oral history is not egalitarian.

I would welcome any constructive suggestions and critical comments on how racism could be confronted in similar circumstances. I must add, as a further complication, that most of the racist remarks were made by a woman who had earlier trusted me enough to make me the first person she had told about her adult feelings as an incest survivor. Having continual reservations and feeling ambivalence about the situation is neither constructive nor politically adequate. It is destructive if I simply feel bad or try to alleviate my conscience with class-based arguments. It is inadequate to avoid it.

Problems such as those resulting from the differences between spoken and written words are not confined to oral history. The experience of researching material and then restructuring it into a continuous work always involves the conjuror's trick of managing to include disparate meanings in a single whole. In this case, the 'whole' was a book, the framework into which the memories could be slotted quite neatly (see the thematic organisation of the chapters, for instance), but gaps in individual accounts were left. These were often of difficult and unexpected shapes. The absence of a unified subject – the London woman hop picker – and the presence of fragmentary narrative voices – women – always showed through the memories in their rich and varied forms, even though hopping had provided a common reference point for us all. It wasn't enough to discover what the women, and I, remembered. It became important to know what was happening, why we remembered in that particular way, leaving those particular fractures and gaps in our histories.

That we construct a successful fabrication of the past which we call 'memories' was not a very useful conclusion. What purpose is served by, or why is there a need for, these personalised versions of the past? What or who is enabled or facilitated, disabled or impeded by such constructions? Were the social relations of class, gender and race being served yet again?

The past–present relationship in the mediation of memory was highlighted again by these questions. But as the Popular Memory Group has pointed out in its critique of the oral historical methodology described by Paul Thompson (see bibliography), the analysis of the past–present relationship can be inherently reactionary:

> . . . the past–present relation appears (in this analysis) mainly as a problem – the unreliability of memory. There is a model of memory at work here and it is a particularly passive one. Memory is the sedimented form of past events, leaving traces that may be unearthed by appropriate questioning. It is a completed process, representative of the past which is itself dead and gone and therefore stable and objective. Once laid down in this way, memories may certainly cease to be available, but this too is a technical problem . . . The most conspicuous absence in such accounts is the present conjuncture in which oral witness is actually recorded. The present is absent both as source of determinations on and meanings of the stories that are told and as the location of current responsibilities and needs . . . Their stories are necessarily influenced by present events and by restructuring of what it is possible to think and say. Oral history testimonies do not form a simple record, more or less accurate, of past events; they are complex cultural products. They involve interrelations, whose nature is not all understood, between private memories and public representations, between past experience and present situations.[5]

This is useful, as far as it goes, but as the 'met man' from

Bracknell said, 'It's a prominent feature of human nature to remember good days and forget bad.' Why? Perhaps we only have what Freud called 'retrospective phantasies', memories not from the past but about the past.

Daughters of our Childhood

Lots of the 'good days' the women remembered were from their childhoods. Many of their stories about hop picking were about them being daughters, even if they had picked when they themselves were mothers. Were the women relating what they thought were their most interesting memories or were they voicing a desire for the comfort of their mothers? There was a fairytale quality and a child-like enchantment in these particular recollections: Joey Foot as the Pied Piper, playing his music to lead the singing hoppers back to the farm, a glow worm lighting their way; riding high on your dad's shoulders – a 'flying angel'; baskets full of good things to eat; enormous puddings boiling in the pot; and, of course, the lovely summers that we had in those days.

In our memories, hopping has become part of a pastoral golden age, a utopian past when 'we was all one'. An unspoken conspiracy might as well exist which disallows versions that might spoil this idyll, which might show another reality. When memories of hardship and pain are recalled they are about other people, not us. The harshly defined barriers of the near-feudal relations and the squalor and poverty, have to be accommodated. We deal with some of this by distancing ourselves: it was those poor souls who were unfortunate; it was our mum who helped the others; we didn't have much ourselves, but 'we was all one'.

This occurs to me at a time when a reconstructed past (based partly on half-remembered childhood pleasures) is an immensely popular and successful means of marketing all sorts of commodities. Advertisements offer us products ranging from 'natural' foods to 'classic' footwear in quasi-historical retail outlets. The pseudo farmyard and the mock gentlemen's outfitters situated, unashamed in their incongruity, side-by-side in the vastness of the suburban shopping mall. Even if we are not old enough to have joined the first time round, we can now be Ovalteenies.

Chain stores, set designers and actors show us, through the soft focus lenses of nostalgia, that this cosy world can be purchased by us, right now: lifestyles, straight out of the magazines; bucolic fantasies for sale, country living in Panama hats. We had values then, security and comfort, and even though we were poor, we shared what we did have. We made our own fun in those days.

Our desires were met.

So we sit alone in our front rooms, our 'Victorian' conservatories if we have them, watching the same advertisements and the same family sagas on our individual television sets. We admire the communality of the past, bathing ourselves in its warm glow, borrowing from its visual vocabulary when we create our homes, celebrating that wonderful time – whether it meant street parties or garden parties. We can choose how we live it now – if we can afford it, or if our credit is good enough.

The poetic resonances, the romanticised appeal, cannot be dismissed easily. They have an undeniable attraction when compared with the alternatives of 1990s' isolation. Women disinherited by age, gender, social and political change, choose cottage neighbourliness in preference to high-rise loneliness.

The present is so awful for so many people – the result not just of the loneliness of dispersed communities and of becoming devalued in old age, but, for growing numbers, of cardboard cities, over-stretched social services, and an ailing National Health Service, all forming part of their lived, everyday reality. Is it any wonder that we yearn for something better? When our memories are so joyful the past can represent a powerful alternative, an escape to the sunlit place where we was all one. The present has failed us. The sanitised past as experienced in our trips around theme park Britain can reign victorious.

The market research organisation Mori was commissioned by

The Sunday Times to conduct a poll on moral standards in contemporary Britain. The following extract is from an article written by Simon Jenkins to accompany the published results of the poll:

> The idea of a country declining into immorality may be a national cliché. Yet it is stated as a fact by a majority of Britons. They feel threatened by some looming incoherence. They long for a golden age of yore. They read of yuppies on the rampage in the City, of stabbings on the Underground, of lager louts battling police in market towns, of fare-dodging, Vat fraud and insider dealing. They sense what Prince Philip has called 'an avalanche of lawlessness threatening to engulf our civilisation'.
>
> Beyond lie darker forebodings: that this decline may be due to precisely the sort of community we are struggling to create, one founded on individualism, acquisitiveness and wealth.[6]

No matter that, for most of us, our experience is of a reasonably safe world, the tabloid press tells us that we are self-deluding fools. Our urban paranoia is inflamed, and we wait, knowing that the mugger is out there, waiting for us in the shadows. Like Chicken Licken, they tell us, 'The sky's falling! The sky's falling!' And we have listened.

When adults feel powerless we shouldn't be surprised that they long for their mothers. Margaret Thatcher has told us that there is no society, only individuals. The free market is their playground. But we *yearn* to be social; we know we can't survive alone. Our rural dreamscape has become the urban nightmare. Or, has the urban nightmare created the rural dreamscape? A chintz safety net. The final irony: Victorian design being embraced alongside its values; post-modernism for the masses; style without content; form without meaning. Historical recreation in every sense.

The past as a place is inaccessible, but our unsatisfied longing for the return of decent values and security, no matter how spurious, can be met through memory. We can convince ourselves that things were not always this bad, nostalgia our reassuring sedative.

The purpose in uncovering the lived experience of the past is two-fold: women have an undeniable right to take their place in history, and the uncovering acts as a focus for us all, a literally 'timely' reminder.

Writing, like any creative activity, does not in itself act as an agent of change, rather it brings attention to, takes note of, and provides material for, the theorising of change. It can point out that the imagery of the verdant landscapes of a past England (the countryside I remember as much from the Ealing comedies of my childhood as from going hopping) gains potency when we are powerless. People can, and some do, lay the blame for their helplessness on the alien 'other' who invades their landscape, making it strange, spoiling it, transforming their beloved (if empty) chapels into exotic places for the worship of foreign gods. There is no church clock any more to tell the community if it's four o'clock. And even if they've never participated in that most image-laden English ritual of high tea, and honey is an unaffordable luxury on their fixed budgets, the resentment of its absence is symbolic of the loss of the past and the betrayal of the present. The Londoners are transformed into home dwellers objecting to the presence of the 'dirty foreigners'. Our unmet desires confirm the past in its role as our ideal community.

But this version of the' past fails to acknowledge its restatement and reinforcement of the social relations of the time when men were men and were paid accordingly. They got the pole pullers' wages while women did the piece work. The past can be a dangerous place for women.

We must continue to think about the lived reality of the past, as well as the meaning it has for those who remember it. By observing, listening and reading the testimonies, rather than judging them, we can share the women's way of seeing the world. This is not voyeurism but a privileged glimpse made possible by their generous agreement to share their stories.

However it is *only* a glimpse, and we must remember that our view is partial. We lose our critical awareness if we simply gawp at the exotic. We should always be aware of the danger of focusing on the honeycomb and failing to recognise it as somebody's lunch.

Notes

1 Quoted in the front of each issue of *The Journal of the Oral History Society*.
2 Thompson, p. 226.
3 Porter, p. 184.
4 'The Peculiarities of Oral History', *History Workshop Journal*, No. 12, pp. 99–100.
5 CCS (ed. Johnson et al), p. 241.
6 *The Sunday Times*, 8 January 1989.

The Women: Biographical Details

The women were generous with their time and always very kind to me when I visited their homes. They were also courageous when talking about some of their ordeals. One woman spoke about her horrifically violent childhood, and the incest she suffered, for which her mother was imprisoned for several years. Her mother was brutal and alcoholic, forcing her daughter to undergo degrading and agonising sexual abuse. When this was discovered at last, she was taken by her grandmother with whom she lived in a converted lorry on a gypsy site. As she said:

> The times I was with my nan, hopping and that, and the last few years, are really the only happy times of my life. Although I still can *never* forget some of the vile things that have happened to me. [Pause] I've not had a good life. I spent so much time in and out of hospital over what my mum kept doing to me . . . But if I was to smell a hop now, I'd be right back. I can see me nan behind the bin and I'm riding off on the tractor . . .

The following biographical details are of the people who agreed to their extended interviews being taped during our meetings. They have been identified by fictitious initials to respect the confidentiality of which they were assured. It is also for reasons of confidentiality that I have not included photographs of the women whose testimonies I recorded.

I have not included details of the many other people who helped me with their time and memories during the research. These people include, for instance, those to whom I spoke on the telephone but did not meet; people who wrote to me; people I spoke to informally (i.e. not during taped sessions); and, of course, members of my immediate and extended families.

Mrs D
Born in London E13 in 1926. Fourteen brothers and sisters. Left school aged 14, but usually only attended in the winter months. Worked as a casual agricultural labourer and factory hand. Married at 21 years. Husband a general dealer. Three children. Last picked about 10 years ago.

Mrs M
Born in London E1 in 1911. Ten brothers and sisters. Left school aged 14. Worked as a sewing machinist. Married, no date. Husband a skilled worker. One child. Last picked 1945.

Mrs S
Born in London E14 in 1919. Eight brothers and sisters. Left school aged 14. Worked as a sewing machinist. Married at 21 years. Husband a dealer and lorry driver. Two children. Last picked about 25 years ago.

Mrs R
Born in East Ham, E6 in 1937. Three sisters. Left school aged 15. Worked as an office junior, cleaner and general domestic. Married at 19 years. Husband a factory worker. Three children. Taken hopping throughout her girlhood.

Mrs AB
Born 'near the Old Kent Road way' in 1917. Thirteen brothers

and sisters. Left school aged 14. Worked as a factory worker and cleaner. Married at 25 and 62 years. Four children. Husbands a gardener and a brewery labourer. Last picked late 1960s or early 1970s.

Mrs T
Born in West Ham, E15 in 1921. Two brothers. Left school aged 14. Worked as a factory worker. Married at 25 years. Two children. Husband a factory worker. Last picked: we were unable to be sure, but after some discussion Mrs T and I thought that she was probably in her late teens when she last went hopping, at approximately the beginning of the Second World War.

Mrs AA
Born in Dartford, Kent in 1951. Mrs AA wanted it known that she counts herself as a 'Londoner', even though a series of increasingly difficult circumstances had resulted in her mother being admitted to a hospital for the mentally ill in Kent. Mrs AA's mother was kept in the hospital during her pregnancy and for several weeks after the birth of her daughter before being allowed to return to London. One stepsister and one step-brother. Schooling: 'Not very much education in the schooling sense.' In care until aged 16. Worked as a shop assistant, fork lift truck driver and office worker. Married at 18 and 29 years. Husbands a driver and self-employed. Three children. Last picked in 1985.

Mrs C
Born in East London in 1909. Eleven brothers and sisters. Left school aged 14. Worked as a sewing machinist and cleaner. Married at 23 years. Husband a dock worker. Three children. Last picked in 1986.

Mrs ML
Born in East London in 1944. Three brothers. Left school aged 15. Worked as a factory worker. Married, no date. Husband a factory worker. Three children. Last picked in 1986.

Mrs B

(Ex-shop owner.) Born in Farnham, Surrey in 1909. Mrs B's family moved to East London soon after she was born. One sister. Left school aged 14. Worked as a factory worker and shop owner. Married in 1933. Husband a reptile dresser (sic) and factory owner and bought the shop which Mrs B ran. Never picked hops.

G

Gilda O'Neill. Born in East London in 1951. One brother. Left school aged 15. Worked as an office junior, general office worker, student and teacher. Married at 20 years. Husband – professional. Two children. Taken hopping until 10 years old.

Bibliography

Beddoe, Deirdre, *Discovering Women's History*, Pandora, London, 1983.

Bignell, Alan, *Hopping Down in Kent*, Robert Hale, London, 1977.

Burgess, A.H., *Hops: Botany, Cultivation and Utilisation*, Interscience Publishers, 1964.

Centre for Contemporary Cultural Studies, ed. Johnson et al, *Making Histories: Studies in History-writing and Politics*, Hutchinson Educational, London, 1983.

Clinch, George, *English Hops*, McCorquodale, London, 1919.

Cockburn, Cynthia, *Brothers: Male Dominance and Technology*, Pluto, London, 1983.

Cohen, Stanley, *Folk Devils and Moral Panics*, St Martin's Press, New York, 1980.

Farley, J., *Pull No More Poles*, Faith Press, 1962.

Janet, Ron, Charles and Peter, *Happy Hopping Days*, Tunbridge Wells Adult Literacy Centre, 1984.

John, Malcolm, *Bygone Hop Picking*, Details of publisher and date of publication not known.

Lewis, Jane, *Women in England*, Wheatsheaf Books, Brighton, 1984.

Lewis, Mary (ed.), *Old Days in the Kent Hop Gardens*, West Kent Federation of Women's Institutes, 1981.

Marsh, John, *Hops and Hopping*, Simpkin, Marshall, Hamilton, Kent & Co., 1892.

Matthews, Jill Julius, *Good and Mad Women*, Allen and Unwin, London, 1984.

Oral History Society Sociology Department, *Journal of the Oral History Society*, Women's History Issue, University of Essex, 1977.

Portelli, Alessandro, 'The Peculiarities of Oral History', *History Workshop Journal*, Ruskin College, Oxford.

Porter, Marilyn, *Home, Work and Class Consciousness*, Manchester University Press, Manchester, 1983.

Roberts, Elizabeth, *A Woman's Place: an Oral History of Working Class Women 1890–1940*, Blackwell, Oxford, 1984.

Sargent, M., *St Francis of the Hop-Fields*, Philip Allan, 1933.

Thompson, P., *The Voice of the Past: Oral History*, Oxford University Press, 1984.